At Issue

|Road Rage

Other Books in the At Issue Series:

At Issue

Road Rage

Amy Francis, Book Editor

GREENHAVEN PRESS
A part of Gale, Cengage Learning

Farmington Hills, Mich • San Francisco • New York • Waterville, Maine
Meriden, Conn • Mason, Ohio • Chicago

Elizabeth Des Chenes, *Director, Content Strategy*
Douglas Dentino, *Manager, New Product*

For more information, contact:
Greenhaven Press
27500 Drake Rd.
Farmington Hills, MI 48331-3535
Or you can visit our Internet site at gale.cengage.com

LIBRARY OF CONGRESS CATALOGING-IN-PUBLICATION DATA

Road rage / Amy Francis, Book Editor.
    pages cm. -- (At issue)
    Includes bibliographical references and index.
    ISBN 978-0-7377-6197-9 (hardcover) -- ISBN 978-0-7377-6198-6 (pbk.)
    1. Road rage. 2. Automobile drivers--Psychology. I. Francis, Amy.
TL152.3.R63 2014
363.12'51--dc23
                                                        2013044032

Printed in the United States of America
1 2 3 4 5 6 7 18 17 16 15 14

Contents

Introduction

Incidents of road rage frequently make the news, but the roads are not the only place where people lose their patience with strangers. "You don't need a car to get road rage," explains Shirley S. Wang, writing in the *Wall Street Journal.* "For many people, few things are more infuriating than slow walkers—those seemingly inconsiderate people who clog up sidewalks, grocery aisles and airport hallways while others fume behind them."

Some researchers are calling this "sidewalk rage" and believe the reason people get enraged on sidewalks isn't much different from the rage we witness on the roads. Whether in a car, on a bike, or walking on a sidewalk, people tend to have strong feelings about how others around them should act. When others don't follow their expectations, they become irritated. Maia Szalavitz elaborates in *Time,* "For many residents of New York City, our bodies are our cars. So rather than engaging in 'road rage' against slow or erratic drivers on a highway, New Yorkers descend into 'sidewalk rage,' paroxysms of fury directed at people who exhibit irrational, obstructive walking behavior on Manhattan's crowded concrete."

While sidewalk rage may be primarily limited to life in big cities, pedestrian rage is a problem everywhere, perhaps with more severe consequences.

According to the US Department of Transportation Fatality Analysis Report System, as quoted by psychologist Leon James at www.drdriving.org, pedestrian deaths due to motor vehicle crashes account for 14 percent of all crash deaths annually. Although the law favors pedestrian right-of-way, James warns that at the very least pedestrians must remain vigilant and not rely on drivers to obey pedestrian laws. More concerning, he believes, some pedestrians actually exaggerate the problem by provoking drivers. He explains that when some pedestrians notice an approaching vehicle "they continue walking slowly as if they are alone in their back yard. . . . This is pedestrian rage. It's passive aggressive pedestrian rage. . . . By appearing to ignore the waiting cars, pedestrians intend to annoy the drivers. That's why it's called aggressive. It is also risky and dangerous."

With the traffic on roads and sidewalks exacerbating stress, it's perhaps not surprising that the term "air rage" has also made an appearance on national news outlets. As explained by Emanuella Grinberg, writing for CNN, "Passengers are tired of long lines, baggage fees and last-minute delays. Airline employees and flight attendants could do without the cranky travelers who refuse to wait patiently, turn off cell phones or stay in their seats. Sometimes that frustration escalates into 'air rage.'" She states that according to the International Air Transport Association, international reports of enraged passengers rose nearly 30 percent between 2009 and 2010, following an almost equally large increase (27 percent) in the preceding year.

Grinberg explains that the rise may be due in part to greater awareness of security threats post–9/11 as well as less expensive flights, which have cut costs in every area from in-flight snacks to the amount of legroom between rows of seats.

In an effort to understand why some people are able to control their feelings and others lash out either on the road, the sidewalk, or in the air, some scientists point to "intermittent explosive disorder," which is defined by episodes of unwanted anger. According to the National Institute of Mental Health, intermittent explosive disorder may affect as many as sixteen million Americans—or approximately 7 percent of the population.

Ronald Kessler, professor of health care policy at Harvard University and one of the authors of the report on intermittent explosive disorder published in the *Archives of General Psychiatry*, stated in a 2006 National Public Radio interview,

"A lot of them are out there on the road, but there are more of them that are in the house. That when you ask these people, tell me about your last attack, the vast majority of them are people who had these things behind closed doors, in their own family; and their spouse or their kids were the subject of their anger rather than strangers."

Intermittent explosive disorder and other possible causes of road rage, the likelihood of finding oneself the target of someone else's anger, and possible legislative and technological solutions to the problem of road rage are all explored by the authors of the viewpoints in the following pages of *At Issue: Road Rage.*

1

Road Rage Incidents Are Increasing

Adam Carey and Jason Dowling

Adam Carey is the transportation reporter and Jason Dowling the city editor at The Age, *a Melbourne, Australia, news organization.*

Australia has seen a steep increase in road rage incidents. While it's unclear where the government can step in to prevent road rage, there are tactics drivers can use to avoid becoming enraged or becoming a target of someone else's rage. Using simple courtesy and having more tolerance for other drivers' mistakes can go a long way toward making the highways safer. Although surveys show that people are aware of how they should respond to other drivers, statistics reveal that they do not always respond appropriately.

When 3700 Australian drivers were surveyed by AAMI [an Australian insurance company] in 2012 about their experiences with road rage, 13 per cent said they had been deliberately forced off the road by another driver. The car insurer conducted the same survey in 2011 and the figure was 10 per cent.

Last financial year Victoria Police logged 212 road rage-related assaults in their database—a startling 42 per cent jump on reported incidents in 2010-11 and easily the highest figure in the past five years.

Clearly Australians are getting angrier behind the wheel, their anger more often becoming violent. Less clear is what is being done to reverse the trend.

No government agency has taken direct responsibility for dealing with the growing problem of road rage. VicRoads [the state road and traffic authority in Victoria, Australia] and the Transport Accident Commission say it is essentially a police matter, and Victoria Police treat road rage as a form of assault or property damage.

Taking another's bad driving personally is the first mistake and often the spark that leads to road rage.

Earlier this month, Paul was driving along Punt Road when another motorist merged into his path without looking. The attack that followed left Paul too afraid to publish his surname for fear of being attacked again.

Paul blew his horn to let the driver know he'd just cut him off. It was the trigger for a frightening attack that rapidly developed from physical intimidation to actual blows.

"I beeped and that, I thought, was the end of that. Unfortunately this fellow had other intentions and tried to ram me several times," Paul says.

The aggrieved motorist then manoeuvred his car directly in front of Paul's, slammed on the brakes and got out of his car.

Buckled into a convertible car with its top down, Paul was a sitting duck. The driver took a swing at his face, which Paul blocked, and then unleashed a string of obscenities.

"Every possible outcome flipped through my mind at that point; how do I escape, do I ram his car, can I ram the car behind me boxing me in, do I swerve into oncoming traffic?"

More verbal abuse followed before the man strode back to his car and drove away. Paul took note of his vehicle number plate and immediately reported the incident to police.

Increase in Offences

Brian Negus, the RACV's [Royal Automobile Club of Victoria] general manager of public policy, is staggered by the increase in the number of road rage-type offences being prosecuted by police.

He says there has to be more "mutual respect" and tolerance on the road; some people's personalities change behind the wheel of the car or truck or on a bike, where they become more aggressive and consider abusing people to be acceptable.

"It is almost like a Jekyll and Hyde syndrome," he says.

David Cuff has been teaching Melburnians how to be better drivers, and to drive defensively, for almost 20 years. The manager of John Bowe Driving in Glen Iris says every day he sees virtually every example of bad driving there is and puts it down to a combination of poor training and bad attitudes.

"I think Australians generally are very average drivers," Cuff says. "From driving in Europe and the US, we're more aggressive generally and we're less skilled."

Being a better driver is as much about attitude as skill, Cuff says. One of the things his school teaches is acceptance that other drivers will make mistakes. Sometimes those mistakes will involve cutting you off, slowing you down, even tailgating.

Cuff says people's attitude towards others changes while they are driving. Two people whose trolleys collide in a supermarket aisle will apologise and go their separate ways. But behind the wheel, those same two people might be more likely to respond aggressively.

In Cuff's opinion, taking another's bad driving personally is the first mistake and often the spark that leads to road rage.

He says if someone does something "dumb," rather than getting upset about it you should accept that they made a mistake.

"You may have done it yourself, pulled out and suddenly there is a car beside you that you haven't seen. You haven't done it on purpose, so if someone does that, instead of getting frustrated and blasting them, think they probably haven't got their mirrors set correctly to cure blind spots."

Cuff's view that road rage can be avoided by simply being courteous and forgiving of another's incompetent or inconsiderate driving echoes the findings of a major state parliamentary inquiry into road rage in 2005.

The inquiry report was described at the time as "the most extensive analysis into the subject of road violence undertaken in Australia and . . . anywhere in the world."

The seven-member inquiry report on violence associated with motor vehicle use, which was co-written by the state's new police minister Kim Wells in 2005, made a dozen recommendations on teaching drivers to avoid conflict, including launching a campaign to encourage greater courtesy. But a courtesy campaign never eventuated.

Following the report's release, VicRoads published a handbook for learner drivers called *Road to Solo Driving*.

James Holgate, VicRoads' director of vehicle and road use policy, says the handbook provides information about sharing the road safely, co-operating with other motorists, and dealing with aggressive drivers. It also gives advice about "keeping your cool in the car," including tips on how best to respond to mistakes by other drivers that don't involve road rage.

In AAMI's latest road rage survey, 38 per cent of drivers admitted to making rude gestures at others for bad or dangerous driving and 19 per cent said they had deliberately tailgated other motorists for the same reason.

On the other side of the aggressive driver's ledger, 70 per cent said they had been subjected to rude gestures and 55 per cent said they had been tailgated. Twenty-nine per cent said they had been followed by another motorist after a heated exchange and 4 per cent said they had been physically assaulted.

Musician Greg Williams was driving east on the West Gate Freeway, at about 100km/h. He was in the outside lane, looking for a break in traffic to move into the left-hand lane and take the next exit, when a man in a 4WD began tailgating him. "He was just really aggressive, and right up my arse, and so I motioned to him to back off and he didn't, he kept on tailgating me and I didn't think it was safe to change lanes," Williams says.

When the 4WD roared past him in the inside lane, Williams "flipped him the bird"—something he soon regretted. The driver suddenly got in behind him, followed him off the next exit and bashed him at the next set of lights.

Violent road rage is not a traffic problem but one of criminality.

"He came straight up to the side of my car, opened my door and started punching me through the open door," Williams says. "I was pinned in the car and he was just pummelling me."

Williams drove himself to hospital and was treated for facial fractures. His attacker was charged with assault. He submitted a written apology to the court and was not convicted. Williams still cannot feel his face properly.

"I remember being anxious driving for a year afterwards, and in the immediate aftermath I was convinced he was going to find me and come and beat me up in my house," he says.

Attempts to Address Road Rage

Driving behaviour experts say violent road rage is not a traffic problem but one of criminality. The 2005 parliamentary inquiry found that most perpetrators of on-road violence were young men, reflecting young men's place as the biggest perpetrators of other violent crimes.

"In Australia it seems that perpetrators often punch or kick their victims or use their vehicles as a weapon to run over their victim," the inquiry found.

It rejected the term "road rage" to describe driving-related acts of violence between strangers, arguing that while the term was widely understood, it was also too amorphous.

The Transport Accident Commission [TAC] carefully considered all the recommendations of the inquiry but found no sound evidence to show that a public education campaign would reduce the incidence of road rage.

Elizabeth Waller, the TAC's road safety manager, says efforts are being made in Victoria to curb road rage.

"The government is addressing road rage with new measures such as fines for tailgating and the successful Roads to Respect campaign. The TAC supports that work by focusing on key contributors to death on the state's roads, including distractions, speeding and drink and drug driving."

AAMI's driver survey found 88 per cent of respondents in Melbourne believed drivers were becoming more aggressive. Of those, 84 per cent said increasing congestion was contributing to that increased aggression.

Andrew Clarke was riding his scooter on King Street in peak hour, using his vehicle's small size to move between cars to the front of the queue of traffic at each intersection.

"This bloke got incredibly upset with that," Clarke says. "When the lights went green, he scooted around the outside of me and then started squeezing me towards the cars that were beside me."

At the next red light, Clarke again threaded his way through the stationary traffic. Enraged, the driver "drove straight into me," Clarke says.

AAMI's corporate affairs manager Reuben Aitchison says the company's latest annual road rage surveys show increasing aggression on the road, and a high degree of intolerance of other drivers. The survey reveals "a massive disconnect" between what people considered appropriate behaviour on the road and how they actually conduct themselves behind the wheel.

"If you ask people what the best response is if someone does something rude or dangerous on the road, about 85 per cent say you should just wave an apology and drive on, even if it's not your fault," Aitchison says. "In reality that doesn't happen. About 47 per cent have verbally abused another driver in response to rude or dangerous driving."

About 54 per cent said they had been verbally abused by another driver.

Michelle Ferlazzo was driving to the city on a Saturday night this month to pick up a friend when an encounter with an angry young man left her shaken.

Ferlazzo tooted the car in front of her at the corner of Royal Parade and Grattan Street in Carlton after it failed to take off when the light changed.

The driver, a young P-plater [driver with a provisional licence], let loose a stream of foul-mouthed abuse.

"He started yelling at me across his passenger. 'What do you think you're doing you f------ bitch? The lights were green for two seconds. What's your f------ problem?'"

Given so many of us are behind the wheel, it should not be so difficult to be more understanding, Aitchison says.

"There are tens of thousands of people on the road at the same time as us, we're all just trying to get somewhere, all trying to find a gap we can get into . . . and we all tend to just take it personally and think it's directed at us. But you've got to take a step back and look at the big picture.

"It's going to slow you down maybe three seconds and it's nothing personal."

2

The Prevalence of Road Rage Is Exaggerated

Rex Roy

Rex Roy is an automotive journalist and photographer based in Detroit, Michigan.

Road rage is not nearly the problem that the media makes it out to be. In Detroit, which was rated as being among the least friendly places to drive, incidents of road rage are exceedingly rare. Further, though reports have blamed driver behavior, particularly inattention, for road rage, more typically road rage is the result of either environmental or engineering issues, which can often be easily resolved. The problem of road rage has been greatly exaggerated.

After watching yet another car whiz past me, while I—and hundreds of other well-behaved Detroiters—waited patiently in a construction zone on I-696 near Van Dyke, I was proud of the general politeness of the other drivers.

There were narcissists, for sure, but none of us who were passed dished out vigilante justice by shooting out the tires of the offending drivers.

This reality presented a sharp contrast to a recent survey I came across. In the annual AutoVantage Road Rage Survey, Detroit ranked as the third most unfriendly city to drive in, behind New York and Dallas/Fort Worth. That consensus came after the Affinion Group survey interviewed about 100 motorists in each of 25 metropolitan areas about driving behaviors on local roads.

"We wanted to identify driving behaviors that could lead to a serious incident," said Mike Bush, a spokesman for Affinion Group. "The common thread that we found is this: In the cities with the worst rankings, drivers simply weren't paying attention to their driving, and this caused problems."

Survey participants noted that this lack of attention—eating, texting, or shaving behind the wheel—was linked with poor driving behavior. Researchers believe this sort of behavior inspires road rage.

In my 30 years of holding a Michigan Operator's License, I've never noticed universally rude and threatening drivers on our roads. Detroit's car culture, I believe, is generally friendly and respectful.

But the Affinion survey begged the question: Is road rage a real danger?

When we go looking for data about the frequency of road rage, there isn't much to support or encourage widespread panic.

So I pressed Michigan State Police First Lt. Thad Peterson about his recollection of such incidents.

"I can't recall a specific incident," he said. "As a matter of fact, in terms of the worst kind of road rage—one that results in a homicide—I can't even recall one ever happening in Michigan."

Road Rage Coverage Is Exaggerated

Like me, Peterson believes media attention to road rage is disproportionate to the reality.

"Road rage makes for great headlines, and upon occasion results in terrible, catastrophic events. But when we go looking for data about the frequency of road rage, there isn't much to support or encourage widespread panic," he said.

Peterson, chairman of a Michigan State Police committee on driver behavior, studies the issue closely.

"We find that aggressive driving is not normally the result of distracted drivers. It is usually the result of some environmental or engineering issue related to the physical roads where aggressive driving occurs," he said.

Factors That Provoke Aggressive Driving

Peterson said major contributors to aggressive driving include: speed limits that are too low for the road; traffic congestion; and poorly timed traffic lights. These act as instigators to drivers speeding, changing lanes and tailgating, all characteristics of "aggressive" driving.

Changes made to roadways where aggressive driving occurs have reduced reported incidents or road rage, he said.

As an example, Peterson pointed to changes made along a section of Interstate 496 outside of Lansing, which accounted for 40 percent of reported incidents of aggressive driving in that area. When the speed limit was raised from 55 mph to 70 mph, incidents of aggressive driving dropped to zero.

"The low speed limit frustrated many drivers, so they drove over the speed limit. This caused problems for other drivers who were driving at the limit. The speed differential caused the tailgating, passing, and speeding that were reported as 'aggressive' driving," Peterson said.

His data also showed accident rates in that area also fell when the speed limit was raised.

Surprisingly, the higher speed limit also improved traffic flow, nearly eliminating all symptoms of rush hour congestion along that stretch.

As the Michigan State Police have pointed out, not-so-obvious factors can cause aggressive driving. More importantly, the scariest incidents of road rage—those we're most likely to read about or see on TV—are rare.

All those people you're sharing the road with may not be perfect, but they're also not likely to go ballistic at the slightest incident.

Good news, eh?

3

Crowded Roads Are the Real Reason for Road Rage

Eric Peters

Eric Peters is an automotive columnist and the author of two books, Automotive Atrocities: The Cars You Love to Hate *and* Road Hogs.

Drivers who have to deal with overcrowding on the road are bound to get frustrated. Traffic congestion is creating longer commute times and there are fewer and fewer areas of the country where traffic flow is not a problem. This problem is only going to get worse as the population of the United States is expected to double over the next one hundred years. Overcrowded roads are the real reason for road rage.

That old nag Dr. Joyce Brothers says that during a road rage confrontation, "men are at the same mental level as an ape," a being who ". . . protects his space, at all costs and without logical thought as to the consequences."

Well, *yeah*.

It's not hard to see how dealing with a driving environment chock-a-block full of cars, many of them driven exceptionally poorly by exceptionally inattentive, inconsiderate and sometimes passive aggressive motorists can make a guy go ape.

People who drive significantly below the posted limit, but who refuse to pull off to the side of the road (it only takes a moment) to let the mile-long line of cars stacked up behind get by; the dude who squats in the passing lane and refuses to move right. The dickweed on his sail fawn; the suburban yenta in her SmooVee. These people create rolling roadblocks, obstructing the flow of traffic—oblivious to other drivers or actively trying to thwart them.

They get a pass.

But it's the "road rager" who, in frustration, executes a passing maneuver on the right or over the double yellow who gets tarred with abuse (and tickets) for reacting understandably to an obnoxious situation. It's never the passive-aggressive left lane hog. He is "doing the speed limit" and driving "defensively."

Dr. Brothers goes on to advise various stratagems to cope with road rage that basically boil down to putting up with the hateful mess that is today's driving environment.

Quaaludes would also work.

The Interstate system . . . is about the same today as it was decades ago. It's hard to even maintain what we have, let alone build new capacity.

The Underlying Problem

No one seems interested in talking about the underlying problem that is ultimately responsible for the road-rageous traffic situation. It isn't poor driver education or bad driving as such. It's simply that America is getting crowded.

Arguably, over-crowded.

Just prior to World War II, for example, the population of the entire United States was less than 150 million. It was still only about 170 million in the mid-late 1960s. But in the past 40 years, the population of the U.S. has surged to more than 300 million today. Looked at another way, we've experienced a doubling of the population it took more than 400 years to build up in less than the course of a single lifetime.

There are many people alive today who were born in a nation with fewer than half the occupants it has today.

According to the U.S. Census Bureau's projections (assuming a modest birth rate and constant immigration levels), we'll be at 390 million by 2050—a short hop in the time-traveling DeLorean from now. That's the equivalent of adding a major city the size of Chicago and its outlying suburban sprawl to every state in this country. Some 2.5 million people (net, after accounting for deaths) are added to the rolls each year—a rate of increase that will cause our present population to double once again in about 100 years.

And these people will be *driving*.

On the same basic road infrastructure designed to accommodate 160 million. The Interstate system, for example, is about the same today as it was decades ago. It's hard to even maintain what we have, let alone build new capacity.

Perpetual gridlock in and anywhere near any major urban area of the country is the result.

It is this endless, inescapable hassle—the constant press of people everywhere—that is at bottom the source of what is generally called "road rage."

Cities such as New York and Los Angeles were isolated islands of congestion as recently as 30 years ago, when even the nation's capital was still a relatively sleepy Southern town and once you got 10 or 20 miles out, you were in the country with not much around but cows and farms. Today, the "greater Metropolitan Washington Area" stretches for 50 miles from downtown and suburbs such as Loudoun and Fairfax County are choked blue with people and cars. It takes an hour or more to travel the 10 or so miles from an outlying 'burb into the city—a trip that took 15 minutes in the 1970s.

We're not yet bulging at the seams with humanity like China or India. But we are rapidly losing open spaces—and open roads—on both the East and West coasts, as well as in most of the South. Cities that were rural cow towns 30 years ago—Phoenix and Denver, for instance—have become major metroplexes just like D.C. and *Noo Yoik*. Indeed, America is fast becoming one vast New Jersey—a paved-over continent of homogenous big box stores, chain eateries and tightly packed McMansion tract housing developments.

"Rush hour" in places like Washington, Atlanta and Los Angeles actually lasts several hours each way—with an ever-diminishing window of reasonably free-moving transportation possible between about 10:30 a.m. and around 2:30 p.m.

It is this endless, inescapable hassle—the constant press of people everywhere—that is at bottom the source of what is generally called "road rage" but which is really just the accumulation/venting of levels of stress that are right at the edge of our ability to deal with.

Axiom: As population/crowds/lines/hassles become more common, so will "rage" of various types.

We are being packed tighter and tighter into a finite space—and compelled to battle one another for scant resources like rats in a Skinner box.

And it is only going to get worse.

Roads Getting More Crowded

Denouncing road rage (or defending it) is not the issue; coming to grips with a rapidly changing America that is becoming a profoundly different place from the one that existed as recently as 20–30 years ago *is*.

The Census Bureau predicts growth rates through the tricentennial (2076) similar to those we've experienced from the WWII era to the present. That could mean 400 million Americans (perhaps more) within the lifetimes of many currently fuming in gridlock.

Just imagine it: 100 million *more* people than we already have. And probably another 100 million cars on the roads.

Even a relatively modest increase in the current population to 350 million or so will forever flush the transportation environment that gave rise to the automobile as a *passion*.

The car culture is dying because driving a car is no longer much fun.

Excepting those living in the handful of states likely to remain relatively diffuse in terms of population concentrations, the idea of buying a 150 mph sports car is becoming the equivalent of walking around in a "Star Trek" uniform and pretending you're in command of the Enterprise, battling Klingons.

What's the point?

"Road rage" can be viewed as the last-gasp thrashing around of the American Dream—a physical rebellion against the loss of open spaces, the ability to go wherever, whenever— and *enjoy the trip*.

4

Hypermiling Causes Road Rage

Michael Rowland and Brendan Trembath

Michael Rowland is a news correspondent and host of ABC
News Breakfast, *a morning news program of the Australian
Broadcasting Company. Brendan Trembath is a reporter for the
Australian Broadcasting Company based in Washington, DC.*

*As Americans deal with rising gas prices, a slow-driving trend
called hypermiling has emerged to help conserve fuel. While hypermiling does save money at the pump, it can be dangerous on
the roads. Slow drivers frustrate others who are trying to reach
their destinations quickly, which often escalates to road rage.
Further, some hypermiling techniques are dangerous, such as
driving below the speed limit, coasting in neutral, or not using
brakes on turns.*

Brendan Trembath: It's the Independence Day long weekend in the United States and many Americans are on the
move.

The American Automobile Association predicted 40.5-
million Americans would be travelling. That's still down more
than one per cent from last year [2007].

Many Americans would be wishing the country was inde-
pendent from the volatile world oil market. The surging cost
of crude has had a devastating impact in a country where the
car is such an ingrained part of the culture.

Thrifty Americans are dealing with rising petrol prices by changing the way they drive.

But Washington correspondent, Michael Rowland, says new driving tactics aren't that popular in the nation's capital.

Michael Rowland: Americans are dealing with pain at the pump in many different ways. Most are just gritting their teeth and pumping away. Others are keeping the car in the driveway and taking the train or bus to work.

The Hypermiling Problem

And then there are those who engage in the increasingly popular practice known as "hypermiling". This involves changing driving habits to get better gas mileage out of your car.

That's doing things like fastening your seat belt and adjusting your mirrors before you start your engine, or turning off your engine when stuck in a traffic jam.

Hypermilers don't brake heavily and when travelling downhill, they put their cars in neutral and simply glide down. But most of all, hypermilers drive slowly, sometimes very slowly.

Driving fast in many cases, dangerously fast, is the norm and heaven help anybody who has the temerity to stay within the speed limit.

By travelling a steady and sedate speed, fewer drops of petrol are drained from the tank and motorists can minimise their visits to the financial black holes known as service stations.

Now driving slowly may work very well in say, Boise, Idaho. But it's fraught with danger in Washington [DC]. Driving in the Greater Washington area is a full contact sport.

Driving fast in many cases, dangerously fast, is the norm and heaven help anybody who has the temerity to stay within the speed limit. There's something about the roads here that transforms otherwise sane and gentle Washingtonians into screaming maniacs.

Citizen Jekyll turns into Fangio Hyde. I've lost count of the times I've been shouted at or gestured at for not driving at 15 miles above the speed limit. Trying to change lanes is a largely futile exercise.

You can spend all morning waiting for somebody to ease on the brakes and let you jump in ahead of them.

Shortly after arriving here I discovered, nearly at the cost of my life, that pedestrian crossings are nothing more than roadside decorations. Washington drivers are just as likely to stop at a set of white lines as they are at intersections where the green walk light is flashing.

So it's of no great surprise that hypermilers are [not] exactly the most popular drivers in this town. Motorists have vented their anger in letters to newspapers.

My favourite is the guy who complained about hypermilers taking off so slowly at traffic lights that they, and maybe only one or two other cars, may make the light. "How inconsiderate," he hurrumphed!

But it's not only the exasperated petrol heads who are having a hard time.

Hypermiler, Glenn Conrad, wrote to the *Washington Post* to describe his recent experience on Interstate 95, the main east coast thoroughfare that snakes past Washington.

Mr Conrad was happily motoring away at 50 miles per hour when he was pulled over by the highway police.

The American Automobile Association considers hypermiling a fad and doesn't encourage it.

"Why was he travelling so slowly?" he was asked. Now, keep in mind 50 miles an hour translates into 80 kilometres per hour.

"I'm saving petrol," he told the incredulous officer. It was an excuse that obviously didn't wash as Mr Conrad was handed a written traffic violation, yes you guessed it, for driving too slowly.

"If you're going 10 miles below the limit, you're a danger," declared the officer. What more needs to be said. . . .

Brendan Trembath: The American Automobile Association considers hypermiling a fad and doesn't encourage it.

It says some of the techniques can be dangerous and should be avoided.

It warns about cutting a vehicle's engine or putting a vehicle in neutral to coast on a roadway, tailgating or drafting larger vehicles, or rolling through stop signs and driving at erratic and unsafe speeds. They say these shouldn't be done.

The auto club has also warned drivers against some maintenance fads, such as over-inflating tires. It says this can improve fuel mileage but can make vehicles unsafe.

5

Hypermilers Need to Be More Considerate

Leon James

Leon James is a psychologist and member of the psychology department at the University of Hawaii at Manoa. His interests include driving psychology, and he maintains two websites on traffic safety and education where he publishes study materials and research reports for scholars, students, safety officials, driving school instructors, and government agencies.

Drivers are bound to react to the mistakes other drivers make around them, but they need to learn to manage these emotions in order to drive safely and pleasurably. A new driving trend makes this even more challenging for drivers—hypermiling. Hypermilers and regular drivers are at odds with one another on the roads as their driving styles often clash. These two groups can share the road peaceably, but in order for this to happen hypermiling drivers need to put more emphasis on considerate driving, which is currently too infrequent a topic within online hypermiling communities.

Driving involves *traffic emotions, traffic thoughts,* and *traffic actions.* These are three independent systems of the driver that need to be trained to work together efficiently. All drivers improve with experience. But this is usually true only about one sector of their traffic actions—handling the vehicle. The majority of drivers do not improve in their traffic emotions and traffic thoughts.

Emotional Driving

Emotional territoriality refers to all the things that the driver cares about and reacts to emotionally.

For instance, some drivers care about how other motorists take care of their car, whether it obviously needs a wash, or repair in a dent, or engine maintenance. This traffic emotion is an extension of the territory of things they care about. Other drivers hardly notice anything about other cars, but they always notice when another driver forgets to turn off the signal, and they have an emotional reaction to it, which is sometimes expressed facially and verbally, for example "Look at that idiot. His signal is still blinking!", which may be accompanied by shaking the head in disbelief, or in disapproval. Overtly aggressive drivers may go even further in the expression of their disdain by yelling at the driver while passing the car.

The yelling and the shaking of the head are traffic actions that result from the cooperation of their traffic emotions and their traffic thoughts. Understanding this cooperation is the key to managing our traffic experience, and improving it so that driving becomes less risky, more efficient, less stressful, more peaceful, more supportive, and even enjoyable and productive.

We need to practice monitoring our mental driving economy. This refers to how we keep track of what's happening around us in traffic. Every moment of driving consists of a loop that we repeat as we drive: Noticing where the other cars are; appraising how you need to adjust to that—like when to slow down or when to pick up; and executing the decision.

Noticing-Appraising-Executing. This is the driver's loop.

Managing Traffic Emotions

Drivers feel overwhelmed by traffic emotions. This causes driving stress and the emotional use of the gas pedal. Both involve costs in higher risk and unhappiness. Drivers can learn to better manage their traffic emotions by monitoring their mental driving economy. This will give them an indication of their emotional territoriality. What are the things they notice about other cars and motorists? How do they react emotionally? What are their traffic thoughts in connection with these emotions?

To achieve effective driver self-management, we need to know what we care about emotionally as we notice things around us.

Knowing their traffic thoughts and traffic emotions, will allow drivers to intervene in the process. The goal is to shrink one's emotional territoriality, to stop extending their emotions to traffic events that do not impact them directly. It involves shrinking one's emotional territoriality by practicing an attitude of latitude. We can notice another driver speeding past us without reacting emotionally. We can experience the sudden fright when someone cuts us off and we have to break quickly. We can't help the emotional reaction, but we can do something to cut it short. We have the choice of choosing traffic thoughts that exasperate and intensify our disapproval of the other driver, or, we can choose traffic calming thoughts. We are in charge of our thoughts much more than of our emotions, and by controlling our traffic thoughts, we control our traffic emotions.

To achieve effective driver self-management, we need to know what we care about emotionally as we notice things around us. We need to monitor the traffic thoughts that go along with the traffic emotions. For instance, you're looking for a parking space and notice one right next to a larger car that is not perfectly aligned. You're annoyed. You feel outraged that you have to either squeeze in, or look for a better stall. If the driver would show up at this point you might glare at the person, or even verbally express hostility. When you think about this scenario from a manager's perspective who is responsible for a fleet of drivers, you would not rank high with such traffic emotions, thoughts, and actions.

In Love with the Gas Pedal

Meanwhile the generation of drivers around did not get or heed this message. With gas cheap and car maintenance affordable, a new driving practice evolved, which can be called the emotional use of the gas pedal. It became an unconscious thing to do for all "normal average" drivers. I have observed that drivers today commonly use the gas pedal to reduce traffic frustrations.

> *Hypermilers and non-hypermilers have evolved into two road user communities that are in conflict with each other behaviorally, emotionally, politically, socially, and morally.*

Many motorists love to hear the roar of their own engines, and love to experience the thrill of acceleration, straight ahead, or around the bend. It feels like a great relief. This relief is an emotional relief. The good feeling is attached to the foot. We begin to love that pedal. We play footsie with it. We press it, and the mechanical monster whirls, roars, and bounces in a faithful dependable response. We are in love with it. It is possessing power in a world in which we have but little, and in which we get tossed around. But the gas pedal gives us power, for a nice change. The gas pedal puts us in charge of things, of how the vehicle is to move and locomote, and even fly (for brief milliseconds anyway).

I observed that when drivers encounter a "left lane bandit" who just refuses to move over, even when being tailgated, they drive around the car in the right lane, as they have no other choice, but they do so by flooring the gas pedal, or using it more than is required for passing. This fuel inefficient maneuver is an emotional defense mechanism, to relieve the negative and explosive traffic emotions occasioned in us by the inconsiderateness of the passive-aggressive driving style of the left lane bandit. We feel inner road rage, and this dangerous traffic emotion is released in a less harmful manner than gesturing, yelling, or cutting off. The emotional use of the gas pedal may save the rageful driver from something much worse and unsafe. Another common instance of the emotional use of the gas pedal is to accelerate and decelerate abruptly whenever some blockage to forward motion is experienced—slower moving vehicle, slow moving pedestrians, traffic lights, stop signs, on ramps, construction zones, coned merge areas, backups,—and now hypermilers. . . .

For non-hypermilers to learn to respect and appreciate hypermilers, they need to experience hypermilers as considerate.

Hypermilers vs. Non-Hypermilers

Hypermilers and non-hypermilers have evolved into two road user communities that are in conflict with each other behaviorally, emotionally, politically, socially, and morally.

Their driving values clash. Their driving attitudes do not fit together smoothly. Their traffic thoughts are contrastive. Their driving goals are dissimilar. Their vehicular behaviors are mutually antagonistic. How is the non-hypermiling driver behind the hypermiler driver, going to experience the vehicle mediated contact?

I have been studying traffic emotions and traffic thoughts for three decades. I can predict that the war between hypermilers and non-hypermilers is going to heat up in the entire range of the driving community—motorists, safety officials, government agencies, advocacy groups, online discussion groups, blogs, and Web sites. We don't want to follow in the footsteps of the terrible war between motorists and bicyclists.

Right now there is still the possibility of a resolution, of peace, between these two groups gearing up for highway warfare. Hypermilers and non-hypermilers need to develop a feeling of mutual respect. Non-hypermilers can admire the tenacity and expertise with which hypermilers perform their fuel efficiency strategies. This requires strong motivation for persisting and being good at it. Americans can admire that. Non-hypermilers can learn some of the techniques used by hypermilers. It's a good thing if we drive with less acceleration and more situational awareness. Crashes at lower speeds are far easier to recover from. Distracted driving is lethal to thousands every year. Hypermilers prompt us to stay more focused on the driving task itself. It remains the main thing to do when driving, instead of dividing attention by multi-tasking with things not directly relevant to driving.

But for non-hypermilers to learn to respect and appreciate hypermilers, they need to experience hypermilers as considerate. This is critical. In the online culture of hypermiling, I found little emphasis or awareness of strategies, techniques, and driving styles that monitor and moderate the effect hypermiling has on the other motorists. This is then a psychological problem between the two camps on the road. For the sake of peace and safety, hypermiling communities need to step up their practices in the area of driver to driver influences.

How one driver acts impacts on hundreds of other drivers. We all know this, but few of us have made it into a focus area for observation while we are on the road and in parking lots. Situational awareness must include conditions, vehicles and drivers.

One of the safest ways to drive is in convoys, with vehicles around you that travel at the same speed, and maintain a relatively safe four-second interval between cars. This style of driving makes events predictable, so that mistakes are avoidable or correctable, as long as the driver is focused and not distracted by other in-car activities.

6

Road Rage and Left-Lane Hogs

John Cichowski

John Cichowski is the "Road Warrior" columnist for the website NorthJersey.com.

Keep-right-pass-left laws are controversial because opponents believe that allowing faster drivers to remain in the left lane—rather than use it only when passing—helps ease traffic congestion and reduces the number of lane changes they have to make. However, the laws are essential to keep slower drivers from hogging the left lane, which only causes more frustration for the drivers who are stuck behind them and increases the risk of accidents as those drivers make dangerous right-lane passing maneuvers. While some blame resistance to these laws for increases in road rage, others worry that increasing education about left-lane hogs could also increase rage.

If you want to start a fight, ask any road warrior this question: Should the laws requiring drivers to keep right and pass left be enforced more strictly?

"Using the left lane only for passing would create even MORE tie-ups," insisted Glen Rock's Michael Leible. "I'd never get to work!"

"They're great laws—for Wyoming, but not a crowded place like New Jersey," said Conrad Macina of Mount Arlington.

John Cichowski, "Road Rage and Left-Lane Hogs," NorthJersey.com, August 15, 2010. © 2010 John Cichowski / The Record (Bergen Co, NJ).

"An artifact of a bygone era!" railed Bill Malville of South Belmar.

The Problem with Keep-Right Laws

Maybe. But police say large-scale resistance to keep-right-pass-left laws is creating unnecessary stress, road rage and crashes, especially when drivers think left-lane hogs are driving too slow.

"Some people won't pull over for police cars!" said Paramus Deputy Chief James Sheehan. "They think they have a right to hog the left lane at low speeds—and that causes road rage."

[The keep-right-pass-left law] enforces lane discipline and safety through "mode separation," a term for separating slow drivers from faster ones.

Like Sheehan, we've all seen this stomach-churning scene play out: A driver stays in the left lane at the speed limit or less, with a tailgater pursuing him relentlessly until he speeds up or changes lanes—two maneuvers that one traffic cop calls "mind boggling."

"The left lane clogs while the center and right lanes have significantly less traffic," he said. "It's as if people are purposely doing the exact opposite of what they should. The entire highway slows down, too, and emergency vehicles can't get through."

Keep-right-pass-left is "an excellent law," said Rutherford driving school instructor John De Giovanni. "It's what we teach all our students." The reason: It enforces lane discipline and safety through "mode separation," a term for separating slow drivers from faster ones.

But in an informal poll, most Road Warrior readers accept only the "pass-left" half of the "mode separation" equation.

"I don't stay right because it's slower there," said Teaneck's Bob Sandler, "and I don't have to deal with cars entering and exiting the highway on the right."

"It's much more dangerous to keep changing lanes to pass slower cars and trucks," said Carolyn Stefani of Bergenfield.

For Ridgewood's Mel Freedenberg, there's only one reason to stay right: "Police are more on the lookout for cars in the passing lane."

Police added this wrinkle to the equation, too: Some immigrants come from places where driving is done on the left, so they're used to passing on the right.

Officially, police insist that they enforce the keep-right-pass-left laws. In the last 12 months 29,245 drivers were ticketed for passing illegally (Statute 39:4–85) and 14,654 received summonses for failing to keep right (39:4–82), according to the state Administrative Office of the Courts.

But only 233 tickets—less than 20 per month—were issued for failing to give way to faster drivers in the left lane.

Why?

"Circumstances aren't black and white," one cop explained. "That's why we have discretion."

If Shore traffic is stop-and-go with too many cars and minimum space between cars, he said, it's a rare cop who enforces the left-lane-hog law. But if traffic is moderate and a driver goes slower than 55 mph, the slowpoke will likely be ticketed "because he's impeding traffic flow, and the hotheads begin taking chances by passing on the right."

What's the Solution?

A 2009 California study suggested taking a fresh look at the American concept of consistent speeds on our superhighways. It said Americans could learn much about lane discipline from German autobahns, where some lanes carry cars at very high speeds while others carry them at prescribed speeds. Low fatality rates under the German system may "explain why accident rates of [American] freeways are consistently lower than those of [local] streets," said researcher Reinhard Clever, "even though speeds are higher on freeways."

Failing such a radical infrastructure change here, police and road safety experts suggest an equally radical attitude change.

"Since the problem is ignorance and arrogance," said Sheehan, "the only way to combat it is through driver education."

Police usually interpret driver education as heightened enforcement, which generally occurs at peak-travel holiday weekends. This strategy would have more merit if it were supported by a more consistent re-education program: Driver retesting tied to license renewal.

If doctors and cops must take periodic courses to maintain their skills, is there any good reason why road hogs, immigrants and everybody else who drives a 3,000-pound machine shouldn't be given the same opportunity?

Or would the prospect of increased knowledge create even more rage?

7

Drivers Who Ignore Left-Lane Laws Fuel Road Rage

Melissa Preddy

Melissa Preddy is a Michigan-based writer.

The left lane should be used only for passing. Drivers who stay in the left lane, particularly at low speeds, are breaking the law. They create dangerous driving conditions by enraging other drivers and forcing them to pass on the right. This problem is so prevalent that websites and products devoted to the issue are rapidly gaining popularity.

If you've ever fumed, fretted and nearly frothed at the mouth while stuck behind a pair of slowpoke drivers riding abreast, oblivious or uncaring that they are blocking both lanes of a freeway, you probably can relate to the level of rage-inducing frustration that has driven other motorists to create websites like SlowerTrafficKeepRight.com and even products devoted to the problem of the left-lane hog.

Left-Lane Hogs

The annoyance is so acute that I found members of an online psychology forum discussing what's up with those discourteous drivers. Some opine in a scholarly manner that such motorists likely are self-absorbed, lacking empathy and unaware of the world around them. Other posters abandon professional decorum, merely wailing "Whyyyyy????" and piling on about the appropriate fate of those who monopolize the left lane. Their ire is palpable.

The problem of passing-lane hogs has prompted more than a couple of thwarted drivers to produce signage in an attempt to alert the slowpokes to proper roadway manners.

J.A. Tosti of Washington state operates Left Lane Drivers of America (LeftLaneDrivers.org), which sells a variety of windshield-mounted decals that order drivers ahead to "move over," with a large arrow pointing toward the right lane. Like the signage on the front of ambulances, the writing on the decals is reversed so it'll be readable by those glancing in the rear-view mirror. He says the perforated vinyl stick-ons are barely visible from the driver's side of the windshield yet easy for cars up front to read.

Left-lane hogs not only are the bane of many commuters' mornings, they are breaking the law.

If they ever do. In my experience those drivers are hunched tensely over the wheel, fixated on the road ahead, clearly out of their element by being on the highway in the first place. Or they're jabbering away on a mobile phone, like the catering truck that abruptly pulled ahead of me into the left lane last week; she was driving about 30 mph slower than prevailing left-lane traffic but that didn't faze her; as I whipped around on the right to avoid a collision she was comfortably slumped against the window, phone to ear, tooling along without a care for the big bottleneck she produced in a rush-hour stampede.

Tosti, a publisher by trade, tries to give left-lane drivers the benefit of the doubt—to a point.

"Some people feel more secure there—even though they are driving 10 miles under the posted speed limit," he noted. "It's a temptation for insecure drivers to stay out of the right lane, because they are afraid of merging traffic."

Nevertheless, Tosti relishes the success of his windshield signs, which went on sale three years ago. Sales are modest, but results are gratifying.

"Sometimes you feel like you're just sweeping the left lane clear," he said.

Slow Drivers Are Dangerous

To those who've lived with the frustration, here's one morsel of solace: In the eyes of state troopers, you, the would-be faster driver, are the righteous one.

Left-lane hogs not only are the bane of many commuters' mornings, they are breaking the law, said Sgt. Jill Bennett of the Michigan State Police Traffic Services Section.

"If you're on a road with two lanes (heading in the same direction), you are not allowed to drive in the left lane for any reason except passing," said Bennett. "Otherwise it's improper lane use, and you could indeed be cited for impeding traffic. That's the case on a freeway, on a city street or on a country lane.

"And if an officer sees it, they will definitely pull the driver over if it's obvious they are lollygagging along and not paying attention to their surroundings."

That's good to know but small comfort when you're stacked up 30 deep behind that dreaded scenario, a slowpoke driver who's pulled abreast of the right-lane vehicle and then for some reason decided to match the other car's speed. Some such drivers on message boards and in real life even gloat that they are preventing faster traffic from breaking the law.

Bennett has a message for them: "They are not the police and it is not their job to enforce the speed limit. In many cases the slow driver can be just as dangerous as the super aggressive driver. And they are definitely more dangerous than the driver going five miles over the limit.

"What we try to explain to those (lane-hogging) people is that you are the problem causing other drivers to get hot under the collar and go off."

So slow drivers, please take J.A. Tosti's hint and move over.

As he says, "Our goal is efficient use of the freeways. That way tempers won't flare and people won't get road rage."

8

Marijuana Does Not Decrease the Likelihood of Road Rage

Chloe Johnson and Nicola Shepheard

Chloe Johnson is a reporter at The New Zealand Herald *and a travel writer. Nicola Shepheard is a journalist based in New Zealand.*

Nearly a third of respondents to a poll done by the New Zealand Transport Agency believed it was safe to drive after smoking pot. Some even believed it made driving safer by relaxing the driver and preventing rage. This view was reflected in a video posted on YouTube by Dre Oakley of himself getting high at the wheel to criticize New Zealand Transport Agency's public service announcements condemning driving under the influence of drugs. Authorities stress that drivers should not be complacent about the dangers of driving under the influence of drugs like marijuana.

Everyone should get high before getting behind the wheel of a car. It will stop road rage.

That is the view of Dre Oakley, 25, who lashed out at the New Zealand Transport Agency [NZTA]'s latest drug-driving campaign by posting an expletive-laden video on YouTube of himself getting stoned while driving/doing burn-outs and drifting. . . .

The 1min 30sec video began with Oakley cursing in an Ali-G type accent before using a blowtorch and kitchen knives to apparently smoke pot while driving. The method, known as "spotting", grinds small amounts of cannabis between two hot knives to emit smoke.

"We know this is fully illegal but this is how we do spots while we is driving down the road on the way to work," Oakley said to the camera.

He goes on to do burn-outs and skids around corners and through intersections before saying "the lesson is get high and do drive-bys, and don't be a taxi man because that is bad."

The video, which had just 455 views yesterday [February 25, 2012], was the third Oakley had made in relation to smoking weed and getting high.

Oakley told the *Herald on Sunday* he made the video "for a laugh" and to demonstrate his view that stoned people could drive safely.

But his biggest frustration against the NZTA ads was the behaviour of actors who exaggerated the effects of drugs, he said.

"It's not realistic," claimed Oakley, who said he smoked cannabis every day.

"I'd prefer to see people who get stoned and drive around, not people who are [fake] stoned and get told off by funny people in the back. That's just silly.

"When I get high I don't feel how they describe it, like 'whoa man that's trippy'. It is not like that, it just makes you feel better like when you're thirsty and you have a drink."

When asked if everyone should drive stoned he said, "F***ing oath I reckon everybody should do it, then it will cut down on road rage."

He said drunk drivers were the real danger on our roads, not those under the influence of drugs.

"Alcohol will f*** you up if you drink too much, and then you're messed up and can't do anything . . . you don't want to see someone drive like that but, you see someone stoned, they just have chingy eyes and feel happy about themselves."

His mother, Carol Ann Oakley, said she didn't approve of the YouTube videos. "He is very fragile and very immature for his age, he just doesn't know the consequences of his actions," Carol Ann said. "I understand why he does it but we don't condone it in any way."

Almost a third of 17,200 people who answered a question about dope-driving in an online poll believe it is safe to drive after smoking cannabis and some argued pot makes it safer.

NZTA spokesman Andrew Knackstedt said the video reflected the extreme end of a growing problem on the roads.

"It's a problem that a good chunk of the population is either complacent about or unaware of," Knackstedt said. "The fact that a third of deceased drivers had marijuana in their system speaks for itself."

Dope-Drivers Not Getting Road Safety Message

Almost a third of 17,200 people who answered a question about dope-driving in an online poll believe it is safe to drive after smoking cannabis and some argued pot makes it safer. The poll was part of a New Zealand Transport Authority campaign featuring TV ads that used hidden cameras to film people's reactions to "drugged" taxi drivers played by actors. The ads, alongside Facebook and YouTube pages, Twitter feeds and billboards, want to kickstart debate.

In two separate questions, a quarter of respondents said it was safe to drive home after a night on E [the drug Ecstasy] (1060 out of 4100), and to drive on prescription drugs against medical advice (1500 out of 4200). And of the 20,500 people who answered a question about whether drugs make you a safer driver, 3400 (17 per cent) said "yes."

Strikingly, 67 per cent of the recent pot-users surveyed said they had driven within three hours of taking it. One theme of the online comments in the campaign is dope-drivers think they can handle driving high, even if others can't.

Transport Authority chief executive Geoff Dangerfield told the *Herald on Sunday*, "The current attitudes about the risks of driving on drugs are similar to the views people once had about drink-driving—often complacent, based on unfounded myths or simply ignorant of the facts."

Drug Foundation executive director Ross Bell said policy-makers needed to approach this as an issue of road safety, not law enforcement—tricky when some of the substances that impair driving are illicit. Dangerfield said that once enough people were talking about drug-driving, the focus would shift to addressing common myths.

Aucklander Cailean Copper Darrington, 18, posted this comment on the campaign's Facebook page: "Drugs can affect your driving but it depends on the potency or quantity of the drug you have consumed, it also depends on what kind of driver you are. If we are going to be so strict about drug driving just remember that caffeine is a drug also . . . just sayin. . . ."

Copper Darrington, who works in a timberyard, told the *Herald on Sunday*: "It's more about knowing your limits. I sometimes drink and skateboard but I find that that impairs me a lot more than other drugs would.

"I think alcohol affects your driving a lot more than marijuana does. I'm not saying marijuana can't affect your driving, but it takes a lot more. I think I'd be all right to drive [after a joint] but I wouldn't because it's illegal."

9

Do You Feel "Righteous Rage" on the Road?

Elizabeth Landau

Elizabeth Landau is a health writer and producer at CNN.com.

A sense of righteousness may be what turns a typically mild-mannered person into an angry, out-of-control person on the road. When something happens on the road that a driver perceives as unfair, he may feel his very existence is being threatened, triggering a fight or flight reaction. Anger not only has an impact on our ability to function socially, it is also physically unhealthy. However, if a person is able to recognize it, this overreactive anger response can be unlearned.

You're speeding along on the highway and someone cuts you off out of nowhere. Your heart starts racing, and you pound your wrists on the horn, screaming obscenities only you can hear.

It's one of those moments when you're so angry that you act out of character, transforming from mild-mannered to vengeful person. It's as if something in your brain tells you that you need to fight back.

Instances of frustration are common in daily life, but sometimes it can get out of control.

Four audio recordings capturing a heated argument, allegedly between actor Mel Gibson and his ex-girlfriend, Oksana

Grigorieva, have been released since July 9 [2010] by Ra-darOnline. In the most recently revealed recording, a man threatens to burn down the house. CNN has not independently confirmed the authenticity of the recordings.

Grigorieva and Gibson were scheduled to appear in court Tuesday [July 13, 2010] for a status hearing on a restraining order that Grigorieva filed against him, alleging that he struck her in the face, according to her spokesman, Stephen Jaffe.

Gibson isn't the only one in the news lately who's allegedly been having anger issues. Carlos Zambrano, pitcher for the Chicago, Illinois, Cubs, has been on the restricted list since June [2010], when he had a shout-out with teammate Derrek Lee. Zambrano has finished anger management therapy and participated Thursday in his first bullpen session since the confrontation, the *Chicago Tribune* reported.

The Source of Anger

Anger stems from a survival instinct, experts say. When you feel that someone is threatening your existence, you fight back to save yourself.

A calm, rational person may appear to transform into an angry beast in a traffic jam because of that need to protect oneself, said Dr. Tracy Latz, psychiatrist in Charlotte, North Carolina.

"It gets into this mentality of 'kill or be killed,'" Latz said. "Subconsciously, there's a fear that someone else is going to kill or take power over me."

Combine that with a sense of entitlement and you've got what attorney and clinical psychologist Robert Goldman calls "righteous rage." That's when people feel so strongly they deserve something that it blinds them to the reality of the situation, and they behave irrationally.

"While we live in a world of abundance in our country, it can also create feelings of anger and rage when we get caught up in it. We're not able to step back and see how really lucky and blessed we are," said Goldman, who works for the probation department of Suffolk County, New York.

In making decisions, the frontal lobe of the human brain, which is relatively new in evolutionary history, is instrumental. But the more primitive parts of the brain are involved in anger, Goldman said. Alcohol can inhibit the more thoughtful functioning and allow anger to flood out.

It's important to understand the root of your anger, and use the sense of unfairness to become stronger.

People tend to lash out at family members because they believe those close to them will not abandon them, no matter what, Latz said. A family setting is when people often let their guard down, which can lead to ugly confrontations.

A person's upbringing may reflect how he or she will handle anger in adulthood, she said. If, growing up, parents expressed their anger in an inappropriate way, or repressed it altogether, the child may follow suit later. This is also how abusive behavior gets passed down from one generation to the next, she said.

Deflecting Anger

"You can actually form a belief that this is how it is—we can unlearn that if we begin to be aware of it," she said.

It's important to understand the root of your anger, and use the sense of unfairness to become stronger, Goldman said. Think about how you can deal with the things that make you mad in a more rational fashion.

In the moment, thinking about the consequences of an action driven by anger can help stop you from going too far, he said.

Another approach is to close your eyes and think of something calming—a loved one, a spiritual being, a beautiful sunset or a piece of music that you adore, Latz said. Meditation also helps.

Seek professional help when your anger is interfering with your ability to function in relationships, Goldman said. It doesn't take aggression for such feelings to get out of hand; if you're unable to move forward with your life because you're still mad at someone for something, there's a problem.

One client Goldman is counseling is still stuck on the fact that his mother wasn't invited to a bar mitzvah on the wife's side of the family. The couple is getting divorced.

"Holding a grudge really impacts your relationship, and it's empowering another person to control you," he said.

Anger Can Affect Your Health

Anger isn't just bad for marriage; it can also affect your health. A 2009 study in the *Journal of the American College of Cardiology* found that anger triggers electrical changes in the heart, which can predict future arrhythmias in some patients.

Mark Farparan also has health issues from anger—he has a condition of chronic pain and fatigue called fibromyalgia, and these days when he gets too worked up about something, his energy will be drained for hours. The breathing exercises that he and his wife learned in Lamaze class have helped him calm down in moments of frustration.

Farparan, 52, considers himself "Mr. Mellow" now, but that's not how it always was. When his 12-year-old son was 3, Farparan once got so mad at the child that he punched a door instead of him.

"I started again in a marriage at a late time, and being a father again was kind of rough," said Farparan, who has a 26-year-old from his first marriage and two children from his second. "I guess I was having sort of like a post-partum."

Farparan has not done that again. Beyond the breathing, his mellowing over the past several years has to do with age, he said.

"I don't have much time left on this Earth. I'm not going to waste it being angry," he said.

10

Area's No. 1 Rank in Traffic Delays Leaves a Lot to Curse About

Ashley Halsey III

Ashley Halsey III is a staff writer with The Washington Post.

As traffic congestion increases on Washington, DC's roads, so does driver rage. In fact, almost a third of drivers in the metropolitan area say that they occasionally experience road rage. Congress must take steps to alleviate the burden on the roads by funding expanded public transportation and other transportation improvements.

The rush-hour commute stinks, but you know that. There are too many cars on the road, but that's obvious. What you don't know is that you're twice as likely to encounter someone caught up in a bout of road rage and that nobody in the nation spends more time stuck in traffic than you do.

DC Drivers Stuck in Traffic

The number of drivers in the Washington region who say they frequently feel uncontrollable anger toward another driver has doubled in the past five years, according to a *Washington Post* poll taken last year. Almost a third of drivers said they're overcome with that wild rage from time to time.

One reason for that boiling frustration is contained in a report released Thursday [January 20, 2011], which found that Washington ranks first in the nation when it comes to hours wasted stuck in traffic.

The most sophisticated number crunching done on traffic congestion says the average Washington area driver loses 70 hours a year—almost three full days—crawling along in traffic, tying the region with Chicago for worst in the country. Los Angeles, the perennial king of congestion, comes in third, with 63 blown hours.

The news came in the annual national traffic survey done by the Texas Transportation Institute [TTI], a highly regarded research group based at Texas A&M University.

The nexus of road congestion and road rage might prove tenuous, but the fact that frustration can lead to anger is not. Very often, according to an earlier study by AAA's Foundation for Traffic Safety, the traffic incident that turns violent is "the straw that broke the camel's back" for someone living a stress-filled life.

"Very slow or stationary traffic situations present typical conditions in which driver aggression can be allowed to reach detrimental levels," the foundation concluded.

As traffic has gotten more congested in Washington, the number of people who say they've felt uncontrollable road rage either frequently or occasionally has risen from 22 to 32 percent.

[In 2009] the average time lost to congestion nationwide was 34 hours, up from 14 hours in 1982.

There is something of a silver lining to the news that Washington is at the top of the heap as far as big-city traffic congestion.

"We haven't been hit as hard by the recession as other major areas like Los Angeles," said Ron Kirby, transportation planning director for the Metropolitan Washington Council of Governments. "Maybe we should be happy to be moving up the list because it means we're going a little bit better than a lot of other places when it comes to job growth and the economy."

Overall, the Texas Transportation Institute report concludes that congestion cost Americans $115 billion in 2009, up from $24 billion in 1982 when calculated in 2009 dollars. Engines idling in traffic gobbled up 3.9 billion gallons of gasoline. Nationally, congestion cost the average commuter $808, up from an inflation adjusted $351 in 1982. And the average time lost to congestion nationwide was 34 hours, up from 14 hours in 1982.

Researchers said the depth of the data used in this year's study far surpassed the quality of information used in past years, giving the results an unprecedented degree of accuracy.

Past surveys used traffic volume data provided by the states to calculate the relative degree of congestion in major urban areas. The same information was collected for this report, but a vast volume of data compiled by a private firm also was figured into the mix.

The company, known as INRIX, places data-gathering devices on 3 million trucks, taxis, fleet vehicles and delivery vans. It also offers an iPhone application that provides users with real-time travel information in return for anonymous tracking of the users' travel.

INRIX information, which is used by Kirby's planners, provides a 24/7 picture of traffic patterns, not just the peak-hour data previously available.

"Now we have the middle of the day, too," said Tim Lomax, the TTI researcher who co-wrote the report. "That's of critical importance because that's when freight moves. It's not just about people taking more time to get places, it's about freight and the economy."

Instead of just rush hour, Lomax can now see weekend traffic issues on the Capital Beltway, around malls and for special events.

"When Stephen Strasburg is on the mound, there's going to be traffic backing up around Nationals Park," Lomax said.

"Clearly, in any growing area—and D.C. has continued to grow—you need to build more capacity," Lomax said. "You can do little things like stagger work hours, fix traffic-light timing and clear wrecks faster, but in the end, there's a need for more capacity."

Pete Ruane, president of the American Road & Transportation Builders Association, said the report underscores the need for Congress to move ahead on the six-year transportation funding reauthorization bill that has been stalled for more than a year.

"The report makes one thing crystal clear," Ruane said. "The failure of elected leaders at all levels of government to adequately invest in transportation improvements is taking an alarming toll on American families and businesses. If members of Congress had to sit in mind-numbing congestion every day like their constituents, they might have a greater sense of urgency in passing the 15-month-overdue transportation bill."

The American Public Transportation Association also urged Congress to act.

"There is no doubt that expanding public transportation use is the key to reducing traffic congestion," said William Millar, the association's president. "Congress needs to move on passing a well-funded, multi-year surface transportation authorization bill. Each passing day means a delay in addressing congestion problems which impact individuals and undermine business productivity."

11

Looking to Avoid Aggressive Drivers? Check Those Bumpers

Shankar Vedantam

Shankar Vedantam is a staff writer with The Washington Post.

A study done by psychologist William Szlemko of Colorado State University found that drivers who decorated their cars with bumper stickers and other personal items are more likely to drive aggressively and react with anger when slighted. The reason, scientists theorize, is that when someone personalizes their car in this way, they begin to see it as their personal territory and therefore feel they need to defend it.

Three horrors await Americans who get behind the wheel of a car for a family road trip this summer: the spiraling price of gas, the usual choruses of "are-we-there-yet?"—and the road rage of fellow drivers.

Divine intervention might be needed for the first two problems, but science has discovered a solution for the third.

Avoid Cars with Bumper Stickers

Watch out for cars with bumper stickers.

That's the surprising conclusion of a recent study by Colorado State University social psychologist William Szlemko. Drivers of cars with bumper stickers, window decals, personalized license plates and other "territorial markers" not only get mad when someone cuts in their lane or is slow to respond to a changed traffic light, but they are far more likely than those who do not personalize their cars to use their vehicles to express rage—by honking, tailgating and other aggressive behavior.

It does not seem to matter whether the messages on the stickers are about peace and love—"Visualize World Peace," "My Kid Is an Honor Student"—or angry and in your face—"Don't Mess With Texas," "My Kid Beat Up Your Honor Student."

Hey, you clown! This ain't funny! Aggressive driving might be responsible for up to two-thirds of all U.S. traffic accidents that involve injuries.

Szlemko and his colleagues at Fort Collins found that people who personalize their cars acknowledge that they are aggressive drivers, but usually do not realize that they are reporting much higher levels of aggression than people whose cars do not have visible markers on their vehicles.

Drivers with road rage tend to think of public streets and highways as "my street" and "my lane"—in other words, they think they "own the road."

Drivers who do not personalize their cars get angry, too, Szlemko and his colleagues concluded in a paper they recently published in the *Journal of Applied Social Psychology*, but they don't act out their anger. They fume, mentally call the other driver a jerk, and move on.

Territory Markers

"The more markers a car has, the more aggressively the person tends to drive when provoked," Szlemko said. "Just the presence of territory markers predicts the tendency to be an aggressive driver."

The key to the phenomenon apparently lies in the idea of territoriality. Drivers with road rage tend to think of public streets and highways as "my street" and "my lane"—in other words, they think they "own the road."

Why would bumper stickers predict which people are likely to view public roadways as private property?

Social scientists such as Szlemko say that people carry around three kinds of territorial spaces in their heads. One is personal territory—like a home, or a bedroom. The second kind involves space that is temporarily yours—an office cubicle or a gym locker. The third kind is public territory: park benches, walking trails—and roads.

Previous research has shown that these different territorial spaces evoke distinct emotional responses. People are willing to physically defend private territory in ways they would never do with public territory. And people personalize private territory with various kinds of markers—in their homes, for example, they hang paintings, alter the decor and carry out renovations.

"Territoriality is hard-wired into our ancestors from tens of thousands of years ago," said Paul Bell, a co-author of the study at Colorado State. "Animals are territorial because it had survival value. If you could keep others away from your hunting groups, you had more game to spear . . . it becomes part of the biology."

Drivers who individualize their cars using bumper stickers, window decals and personalized license plates, the researchers hypothesized, see their cars in the same way as they see their homes and bedrooms—as deeply personal space, or primary territory.

Unlike any environment our evolutionary ancestors might have confronted, driving a car simultaneously places people in both private territory—their cars—and public territory—the road. Drivers who personalize their cars with bumper stickers and other markers of private territory, the researchers argue, forget when they are on the road that they are in public territory because the immediate cues surrounding them tell them that they are in a deeply private space.

"If you are in a vehicle that you identify as a primary territory, you would defend that against other people whom you perceive as being disrespectful of your space," Bell added. "What you ignore is that you are on a public roadway—you lose sight of the fact you are in a public area and you don't own the road."

Szlemko said that, in an as-yet-unpublished experiment, he conducted tests of road rage in actual traffic. He had one researcher sit in a car in a left-turn lane. When the light turned green, the researcher simply stayed still, blocking the car behind.

Another researcher, meanwhile, examined whether the blocked car had bumper stickers and other markers of territoriality. The experimental question was how long it would take for the driver of the blocked car to honk in frustration.

Szlemko said that drivers of cars with decals, bumper stickers and personalized license plates honked at the offending vehicle nearly two full seconds faster than drivers of cars without any territorial markers.

12

Road Rage Is Primarily an Anger Problem

Steve Albrecht

Steve Albrecht is a San Diego–based speaker, trainer, and author on high-risk human resource and security issues with fifteen books to his name.

It seems that drivers are getting more territorial and are more easily enraged. Even people who are normally mild-mannered can find themselves enraged behind the wheel. The medical community identifies a behavior as a problem when it has undesired consequences, and road rage, which can lead to reckless driving arrests and violent confrontations with others, certainly fits this definition. Although it's not easy to do, drivers need to develop stress management techniques to avoid falling prey to road rage.

If you need proof we are no longer living in a 24/7 world but more like a 72/7 world, look around the highway as you drive to and from home, work, or school. The current pace of life finds many of your fellow drivers with eyes locked hard on to their phones and their feet stomped heavy on their gas pedals. These days, it's hard not to feel like the drivers to your left and right have become more territorial, more aggressive, and just plain meaner when they get behind the wheel. Is the affliction known as "road rage" a larger symptom of a general anger problem?

You see it every day on our roads: people speeding past; changing lanes with no signal; weaving dangerously across three and four lanes; passing too closely on either side of your car; speeding up to block you out; not allowing you to change lanes or merge on or off the highway; racing other drivers (i.e., two maniacs who think [their] car-handling skills are better than they actually are); roaring up behind as if they might intentionally rear-end you; constant tailgating; horn honking; flashing high beams at your mirror when you are in "their" fast lane; finger flipping; screaming out the window; causing or creating accidents; pulling over to fight; or worse, kill the other driver.

What used to be a largely male problem has crossed gender lines. Women may not get into roadside fistfights or point guns at each other like men, but they can drive just as aggressively, rudely, and even dangerously. It's the rare time when male and female aggression is on display in near-equal amounts. For many men, aggression is supposed to be overt; for women it is more covert. But put them both behind the wheel, late for something, angry about something else, and in no mood for courtesy, and their behaviors will compare.

What factors cause a usually mild-mannered person to see red? Some people who are ordinarily even-tempered admit that they have an easy tendency to lose control of their emotions when they get behind the wheel. Their fuses get lit when they put their keys into their ignitions.

For some road ragers, it's a need for control, to counter to other drivers who they feel violate their proxemic space, or their need for possession of their lane or their part of the road. For others, it's unchecked anger and aggression. It's hormone-based, primitive, small-brain thinking, bringing a lack of emotional intelligence or the need to dominate someone else and their unsharable space. Add in unchecked egos, the need for superiority, narcissistic pride, and male genital one-upmanship: my vehicle is bigger than yours.

Mental health professionals define certain behaviors as problematic when they have consequences. Road rage, and especially those acts which lead to confrontations, can have significant consequences, including getting cited by the police; getting arrested for reckless driving (three or more moving violations in a row); having your license suspended or revoked; losing or tripling your auto insurance policy; damaging your car or the other driver's car; getting sued; or injuring or killing someone in the other car or someone in your car, including your spouse or children. Road rage victims and perpetrators have been pepper sprayed, stabbed, beaten, run down, and shot by each other.

One simple answer to road rage is to simply concentrate fully and intently on your own driving, and not make eye contact or care about the people around you.

The minor consequences are that you continue to let one isolated event on the road ruin your whole day or get you a traffic ticket. And don't discount the not-insignificant matter of embarrassing your family as you act like a spitting, cursing, raving lunatic. If you show that side to your kids too often, they could learn to see that behavior as somehow "appropriate" when they get old enough to drive. Or just as bad, they think mom or dad is an immature ass.

Solutions are easy to say and often hard to follow. Some people don't have the will or wherewithal to try to cure themselves, even under the threat of an injury, a crash, a citation, an arrest, or a lawsuit. They suffer from the "It's the other driver's fault" syndrome. But one simple answer to road rage is to simply concentrate fully and intently on your own driving, and not make eye contact or care about the people around you, even when their own skills leave a lot to be desired.

Another easy tool is to practice stress breathing: inhale for a count of four, hold for count of four, exhale for a count of four, hold for a count of four, and repeat the cycle as many times as necessary to bring your pulse rate and blood pressure back to normal levels.

Perspective is an important part of road rage prevention too. You are you. The other driver is the other driver. Only you can let someone ruin your day or worse, or push your hot buttons. Focus on being "relentlessly positive" and realize you can't control, coerce, or fix other people. You can only manage you. Practice kindness, starting with you first.

WWDLD? What Would the Dalai Lama Do? Go forth down the road and be yourself, with compassion towards others. Stop caring about your "space." Tint your windows. Get a subscription to satellite radio and enjoy your music without commercials. Realize road rage is ridiculous, life-threatening, and not something you have to participate in, ever.

13

Is Road Rage Just Bad Manners?

Michael J. Hurd

Michael J. Hurd is a psychotherapist, life coach, and author who resides in Delaware.

Intermittent Explosive Disorder (IED) is a new diagnostic term being used to explain why some people experience road rage and others do not. Categorizing road rage as a mental health disorder has implications for the legal ramifications of the behavior. Diagnosing anger as a medical problem takes responsibility away from the people who behave badly and need to learn better coping mechanisms. Regardless of whether or not IED should be used as a diagnosis, it should not be used as a legal defense.

More than just another media catch phrase, "Road Rage" now describes one of the more recent "diseases" to be foisted upon us by some members of the mental health profession. To make it a little more official, they've named our latest affliction "Intermittent Explosive Disorder" (IED for short).

According to the National Institute of Mental Health, IED might affect nearly 8 percent of the U.S. population. And though road rage isn't the only form it takes, it is the most easily identifiable. We've all experienced it, either in ourselves or in others. People hammer on their horn, display the proverbial "finger," or shout insults. Or (and this is the important part), you might have FELT like doing these things, but you had enough respect for yourself to not act on those feelings.

It takes more than just getting really mad to qualify for IED. According to the standard psychiatric diagnostic manual, an individual must have had three (count 'em, three) episodes of impulsive aggressiveness "grossly out of proportion to any precipitating psychosocial stressor," at any time in their life. The person must have "all of a sudden lost control and broke or smashed something worth more than a few dollars ... hit or tried to hurt someone ... or threatened to hit or hurt someone." Three times, mind you.

Though some health professionals (and, I'm sure, more than a few crafty lawyers) want to see uncontrolled anger classified as a physical disease, could it really be something else? Like maybe a lack of self-control? We've heard for years about the need for "anger management," implying that people should take responsibility for managing their own anger. They might need professional help, of course, but in the end, a chronically irate person has to take responsibility for curbing his own anger, just as the recovering alcoholic tries to avoid bars, or the compulsive gambler has to stay away from casinos.

The fact that we can't control traffic doesn't automatically mean that we still don't have control over ourselves.

Dr. Emil Coccaro, chairman of psychiatry at the University of Chicago's medical school, begs to differ. "People think [IED is] bad behavior and that you just need an attitude adjustment, but what they don't know ... is that there's a biology and cognitive science to this." He cites a two-year National Institute of Mental Health study that suggested that anywhere from 5 to 7 percent of Americans fit the diagnostic criteria of IED.

OK. So a lot of Americans are angry. Really angry. But does this prove that it's heredity, hormones and biology? Medical science and the field of psychology cannot answer that question. For people who struggle with anger, the solution (like it or not) is attitude adjustment. Using psychotherapy, or maybe just plain old common sense, people who struggle with anger must learn to say to themselves, "I have a choice here. I can explode into rage. Or I can take a deep breath and try to think about it." The difference between an IED person and a normal person is that the IED person has to work harder at improving his attitude. It might not be fair, but the IED person really doesn't have any other choice. There's no pill to make the anger go away.

On the road, it's normal and natural to feel a lack of control. Columnist Eric Peters, writing for America Online, suggests that human beings are not psychologically or biologically "wired" for sitting in traffic. "We were not bred for this sort of abuse. We have not had time to evolve new mechanisms (such as an internal morphine release gland, let's say) to cope with an environment our hunter-gatherer systems are completely ill-equipped to deal with."

It's an interesting theory. And, as it stands, probably true. But the question remains: How are we supposed to deal "in the moment" with feelings of rage that might stem from a sense of being out of control?

People who regularly cope with traffic tell me things like, "I put on my favorite music, or a book on tape." Or they give themselves extra time. Or, "I simply accept what I can't control." Sometimes they plan their activities at less busy times, or even consider relocating. Either way, there ARE solutions; we just have to look for them. The fact that we can't control traffic doesn't automatically mean that we still don't have control over ourselves.

Accepting what you cannot control, and getting to work on what you can control, marks the foundation of successful attitude adjustment. Those who cope better with anger and rage (the majority, according to NIMH) have either success-fully adjusted their attitudes and behaviors, or had better atti-tudes to begin with.

Labeling every distasteful trait and destructive behavior as a "disease" opens up a Pandora's Box of needless medications, ridiculous legal defense strategies, and phony excuses. We can avoid all this by "curing" ourselves through the power of inde-pendent thought and accepting responsibility for our own ac-tions.

14

How to Fight Road Rage

Hal Arkowitz and Scott O. Lilienfeld

Hal Arkowitz and Scott O. Lilienfeld serve on the board of advisers for Scientific American Mind. *Arkowitz is a psychology professor at the University of Arizona and Lilienfeld is a psychology professor at Emory University.*

Road rage is more common than most people realize. Although there are some similar traits among the people most susceptible to road rage, anyone could find themselves losing control behind the wheel. There is, however, treatment available for reducing rage that has been proven effective in research trials. Increased penalties, public education, and changes in car design could also help to alleviate the problem of road rage.

Consider the following recent sobering reports:

- A motorist shot and killed the driver of another car "because he was driving too slowly."

- A large crowd was blocking the parking lot exit of a nightclub. A driver who was growing impatient with waiting for an opening drove his car straight into the crowd, seriously injuring seven people.

- When Jack Nicholson got cut off, the actor waited until both he and the other driver were stopped at a red light, then got out of his car, and hit the windshield and roof of the other car with his golf club. He returned to his car and drove away.

Of course, *you* wouldn't do such things. Or would you?

You might, because road rage is remarkably common. In one survey of more than 500 drivers, 90 percent reported that during the past year they either were a victim of road rage or had witnessed it. These statistics actually may be underestimates. For one thing, many respondents may not want to admit to road rage because it is socially undesirable. Also, more people report being the target rather than the initiator of road rage, supporting the idea that initiators may not be fessing up.

People with aggressive tendencies across a variety of situations, including home and work, have an increased likelihood of road rage.

Psychologist Elisabeth Wells-Parker of Mississippi State University and her associates have suggested that the term "road rage" implies specific incidents of anger and aggression directed intentionally at another driver, vehicle or object. When the behavior erupts, the presence of firearms can worsen the situation. As physician Matthew Miller of the Harvard School of Public Health and his colleagues have pointed out, 11 percent of a randomly selected sample of 790 drivers reported that they always or sometimes carried a gun (usually loaded) in their vehicle.

Who Are These People?

Anybody can be susceptible. Road ragers are men and women, young and old, rich and poor, mentally disturbed and healthy, people with and without generalized anger problems, and members of various ethnicities. Some become angry almost every time they drive, whereas others do so infrequently. Although aggressive retaliation, such as assault or murder, characterizes the extreme end of these behaviors, most crabby drivers engage in milder displays, such as verbal insults, obscene gestures, honking their horn, cutting off other drivers and chasing other cars.

Still, research does point to some similarities among those who are susceptible to belligerent acts when behind the wheel. People with aggressive tendencies across a variety of situations, including home and work, have an increased likelihood of road rage. Younger drivers are more prone than older drivers are. Men have historically displayed a greater predilection, although women recently have been catching up. Many road ragers are otherwise model citizens who are successful in work and in relationships and well respected in their communities.

Regardless of the initiating factors . . . road ragers seem to respond to various types of therapies.

Why do some people get angry and even violent in response to the irritating behavior of other drivers, whereas others do not? Psychologist Jerry Deffenbacher of Colorado State University has proposed that some people have a trait for, or predisposition toward, this type of behavior that is triggered by the poor driving of other motorists. Many of his studies have found that those who display lower levels of the trait are far less likely to respond with road rage, even when exposed to the same triggers.

Other researchers have tried to uncover the nature of this trait, and their studies have found that those prone to road rage may show one or more of a variety of characteristics: general aggression (not limited to driving), high levels of stress, antisocial tendencies, or low impulse control and frustration tolerance. Researchers have also demonstrated that road ragers are sensitive to supposed attacks on their self-esteem. For example, in the clinical practice of one of us (Arkowitz), people with road rage problems perceived the irksome behaviors of other drivers as a sign of disrespect and a personal insult rather than attributing those behaviors to the other drivers' carelessness or recklessness. Arkowitz found it useful to help clients learn that "it is not about you." Certain psychological problems have also been found to relate to the road rage trait, including antisocial and borderline personality disorders as well as alcohol and substance abuse.

It is apparent that road ragers represent a very mixed bag of people. They may have only one of the attributes described above or several characteristics, or they may have other features we have yet to discover. Regardless of the initiating factors, however, road ragers seem to respond to various types of therapies.

Prevention and Treatment

Although prevention is the best option, studies have shown that treatment can be effective as well. Deffenbacher conducted two experiments in which subjects received either training in relaxation only or training in relaxation along with other therapies intended to change subjects' dysfunctional thoughts about driving. In general, subjects did better with either of the two treatments than with no treatment. These studies were well designed, but we need to be cautious about generalizing the results to the wider population because all subjects were college students and thus do not represent the full range of road ragers.

Recently psychologist Tara E. Galovski of the University of Missouri–St. Louis and her colleagues evaluated a group treatment for road rage aimed at adults who were either self-referred or court-referred. Treatment consisted of four weekly two-hour sessions that included education about road rage and anger, recognition of being an angry driver, relaxation techniques, coping skills and training in different ways to think about anger-eliciting driving situations. Those who received treatment did far better than those who did not and curbed their aggressive behavior by more than 60 percent on average.

In addition to combating the problem with treatments for individuals, policy leaders could make changes that might reduce road rage in society at large. Sociologist Mark Asbridge of Dalhousie University in Halifax and his associates have made interesting recommendations. One of these is new or increased penalties for road rage. Laws already cover extreme forms, such as assault and dangerously aggressive driving. Asbridge and his co-workers suggest the possible value of broader adoption of an Australian national law that stipulates that drivers must not drive so as to "menace" other persons by threat of personal injury or property damage. Other ideas include mass-media education about road rage and how to avoid it, societal changes such as reducing traffic congestion and promoting public transportation, court programs for convicted road ragers, and redesign of cars to prevent excessive headlight flashing and horn blowing; some cars have already been designed to prevent tailgating.

We conclude with a brief anecdote. Arkowitz used to drive to work on a road that prominently displayed a billboard advertising a funeral home. It showed a picture of the funeral home, along with five simple, but powerful, words: "Drive carefully, we can wait." We hope that greater awareness of road rage and its treatments will help keep them waiting for a long time to come.

15

Driverless Cars Could Eliminate Road Rage

Gini Graham Scott

Gini Graham Scott holds a PhD and has published thirty books and produced more than fifty short videos through her companies Changemakers Publishing and Writing and Changemakers Productions.

It's only a matter of time until driverless cars are a daily reality, and among the many intriguing questions is how this will affect road rage. For as long as driverless and traditional cars share the road, there will still be rage. However, injuries are bound to go down when there is only a computer to blame. Instead, lawyers may find a new booming business suing manufacturers who sell malfunctioning cars to the public.

The idea of driverless cars may seem like a sci-fi fantasy now, but they are already being tested and driven. And they work, so it's already a matter of time before they begin appearing on our roads. The first of these cars are being tested by Google, as Megan McArdle describes in a *Daily Beast* article: "Are Driverless Cars Really in Our Near Future?"—and in a series of articles on Forbes.com, Chunka Mui, who helps companies design and stress-test their innovation strategies, reflects on the implications of these cars. Among other things, he suggests that Google's driverless car will be worth $2 trillion a year or more in revenues, and it would save millions from reducing traffic accidents, wasted commute time and energy, and the number of cars on the road by 90%. He suggests that driverless cars will dramatically reduce human error, the number one cause of accidents, and people can spend their time in cars enjoying all kinds of entertainment provided by electronics companies and app makers. Plus now the manufacturers will become responsible in the case of accidents, since the liability will depend on "the driving skills of the car" rather than the owner. And very soon these cars will be appearing on the road, especially from Google, now that California recently passed legislation for driverless cars, with backup drivers.

If no one is driving a driverless car, there might be no other person to blame, just the car's faulty software. So the enraged driver might just calm down.

Driverless Cars and Road Rage

But what about road rage? None of the articles I read about driverless cars said anything about that, and I began to wonder how the advent of these cars might affect the growing phenomena of road rage by furious drivers—not only affected by accidents but by the driver's behavior in another car. So far there have been so many of these incidents—about 1,500 people a year are seriously injured or killed in these traffic disputes, and many thousands if not millions more have these confrontations with someone who is raging, that the American Psychiatric [Association] has even coined its own diagnosis. It's known as Intermittent Explosive Disorder and, according to the National Safety Commission, it is characterized by "a degree of aggressiveness that is grossly out of proportion to any influencing events." It is even considered a form of temporary insanity in which the enraged person wants to hurt other people or destroy property, and it's mostly found in young men.

So what happens when a driverless car is involved in an incident that might provoke road rage? Sure, if two driverless cars are in an accident, it's mainly a question for the manufacturers to decide—whose software was at fault, and then the guilty car-maker pays. So no road rage, because no one's driving the car—though perhaps if there's a back-up driver or people enjoying themselves in the back of the car—maybe they could still get mad and jump out of the car to confront any one who happens to be in the other car, and if not, perhaps they might still take it out on the poor defenseless driverless car. Likewise, if one driverless car cuts off another on the road, it's just following the directives from its software, and the other driverless car isn't going to get mad. Its software will just register the passing car.

But what about in the long period of transition, when a car with a real driver encounters a driverless car in an accident or gets angry when such a car cuts it off in traffic or maneuvers more quickly into a parking space on a crowded city street or parking lot? What happens to the feelings of anger that might normally turn into road rage when one infuriated driver is sufficiently riled up to strike out at another? But if no one is driving a driverless car, there might be no other person to blame, just the car's faulty software. So the enraged driver might just calm down, though perhaps in some cases, take aim at the car with a good kick, bat, gun, or other object.

Thus, at least actual injuries and deaths due to road rage are likely to go down, since these encounters will involve two driverless cars who can't attack anyone—just record whatever happened on their onboard cams. Or if the encounter pits someone driving a real car against a driverless car, the angry individual will have no person at fault—just a car with no one at a wheel—which might be the end of the incident, since it can be hard to get or stay mad at a car, or at most the person might beat up on the car, which can't fight back, though the risk is having every [act] recorded on video. Or then again, maybe attacked cars might be programmed to respond back if attacked, say by having folded up knives and pincers like the cars of the future in sci-fi films do. So if anyone dares to attack—watch out, the car might zap you back, which might discourage road rage, too.

In any case, it would seem on balance there's likely to be much [less] road rage as more and more driverless cars hit the road. But the likely alternative is a bonanza for lawyers who can now sue the manufacturers with lots of money for any errors in the software in these new driverless cars—which is likely to be much more than anything obtained due to limits on insurance or drivers who have less money. In turn, this might trigger a new kind of rage. Call it "driverless liability disorder" or DLD, and maybe the American Psychiatric Association may come up with an official diagnosis for that, too.

16

Driverless Cars Will Not Solve the Problem of Road Rage

Digital Trends

Digital Trends *is a web-based technology news publication that reviews products and provides articles about the ways in which technology is changing our lives.*

Driving errors will not be eliminated by driverless cars. At a 2013 technology conference in Las Vegas, researchers demonstrated how the computers in driverless cars could be hacked to make them drive erratically and dangerously. Although the new technology may eliminate driver error, it won't likely make the roads any safer. As some states are already legalizing automated cars, the future of these machines still remains uncertain at best.

If I've said it once, I've said it a million times: Real cars died the day we stopped installing carburetors and started packing the things full of as many computer modules as possible. And now, just like clockwork, our Frankenstein monsters are coming back for their revenge.

Hacking Car Computers

Signs of the trembling undead showed up last month, when Twitter security researcher Charlie Miller—who, you might be interested to know, is also a former NSA [National Security Agency] hacker—and IOActive's director of security intelli-

gence Chris Valasek revealed that they had successfully wea-
seled their way into the computer systems of Ford's Escape
and Toyota's Prius.

As Miller and Valasek explained in a downright whimsical
talk at DefCon [annual hacker convention] on Friday [August
2, 2013], by burrowing down into the cars' array of electronic
gizmos, the pair has figured out a way to successfully take
control of the brakes, steering, acceleration, and even the seat
belts of these cars. And they aren't talking about the kind of
helpful control that allows my neighbor George to drive de-
spite not having any arms.

"I think this is where we almost died, right there," joked
Valasek, as he showed off a video of Miller nearly losing control of his hijacked Prius to DefCon. The crowd, of course,
just laughed and laughed.

Listen, I like jokes as much as anyone. I mean, have you
ever seen Carlos Mencia? That guy knows how to lay down a
punch-line. Look him up sometime. Know what isn't funny?
Vehicular homicide. And now, thanks to Miller and Valasek,
thousands of ambitious DefCon dweebs have the know-how
to turn our cars into high-speed killing machines. The problem is so serious, most of us will soon be dreaming of the
good ol' days when the scariest things on the road were old
people and Asians. *(Ed note: Mr. Worst Case Scenario [pseud-
onym of author of this essay] does not represent the views of
Digital Trends.)*

I only wish this story ended here. But the future, it seems,
holds a whole new set of terrors.

Next on stage, a renowned Australian hacker known as
Zoz summed up the situation: "I'm a huge fan of unmanned
vehicles. I love robots, I think they're the future. . . . But, like
everything else humans have ever made, these systems are going to get hacked."

According to Zoz, who spends much of his time fiddling around with our future overlords, society is hurtling toward a future in which robots, from military drones to civilian unmanned aerial vehicles to Google's driverless cars, do much of our transportation for us. "Look at all the advantages," he cheers. Zoz even had the gall to create a robot pizza delivery bot—because what America needs right now is more contraptions stealing our jobs.

Every single one of these systems can malfunction—or, worse, be tricked into doing something deadly.

"The revolution is coming," says Zoz. "You can't stop it, even if you want to."

After his talk, I've never wanted to stop the robot revolution more—especially when it comes to driverless cars.

See, autonomous vehicles use a dizzying array of sensors, maps, GPS, and other clues to avoid flying off a cliff or driving in through your front door. And you might think all that high-tech whizz-bang trumps some jackass hurtling down the road at 60 while texting pictures of his junk. Thing is, says Zoz, every single one of these systems can malfunction—or, worse, be tricked into doing something deadly.

GPS can be jammed or spoofed. Laser range finders can be rendered worthless by tossing a bit of dust or smoke in their path. Millimeter wave radar can't even handle reflective puddles or even shiny "new asphalt," says Zoz, without promptly slamming on the brakes, or driving the vehicle straight through whatever it thinks isn't there. Maps can be remotely manipulated by crafty hackers. And cameras are damn near useless.

Zoz showed off a slew of examples of unmanned vehicles malfunctioning in frightening ways: Driverless cars flying off roadways and catching on fire. Driverless vans driving straight over Jersey barriers. Driverless SUVs plowing into buses full of blind orphans. Okay, that last one didn't happen—but give it time. Such carnage is inevitable with these four-wheeled terminators.

Then, as if on cue, Zoz busts out with perhaps the most disconcerting fact of them all: "Here's the key thing," he says. "When designers watch the robot in action, they don't necessarily know, even though they programmed the whole thing, why it's doing what it's doing."

Everyone likes to say that driverless cars are the future. That they'll be safer because they remove the possibility of human error. Turns out, these contraptions will have human error baked right into their soulless hearts.

Robot Rage?

Just as Zoz started going off on "robot road rage," I had to flee the room due to a panic-induced asthma attack. I burst outside, and onto the street. As I stood in the oven-like heat, cars buzzed passed me along West Flamingo Road. And then I remembered: Nevada has already legalized the deployment of these unmanned contraptions. I have less than 48 hours left in this hellhole. Here's praying I make it out alive.

Over and out.

17

"Road Rage" Case Highlights Cyclist vs. Driver Tension

Mandalit Del Barco

Mandalit Del Barco is a national correspondent with National Public Radio (NPR). Her news reports, feature stories, and photos filed from Los Angeles and abroad can be heard on various NPR programs.

Many cyclists ride in fear of being injured by a car and complain that reports of road rage against them and even crashes are not taken seriously by the police. However, a crash in July 2008 involving two cyclists and a car resulted in the car's driver being convicted of six felonies, including assault for using his car as a deadly weapon. This is widely considered a landmark case for protecting cyclists who are frequent victims of road rage from drivers who resent having to share the road.

*B*icycling magazine called it "the road rage incident heard 'round the cycling world."

A driver in Los Angeles was recently convicted of using his car as a weapon against two cyclists. And the case is focusing attention on the often uneasy relationship between motorists and bicyclists who have to share the road.

It happened last year on the Fourth of July, on a steep, narrow road in L.A.'s Mandeville Canyon. Cyclists Christian

Stoehr and Ron Peterson were riding side by side when a doctor who lived in the neighborhood came up from behind in a sedan.

"There was an exchange of words," Stoehr recalls. "He then accelerated within five feet in front of us, pulled over and slammed on the brakes."

Stoehr says there was no time for them to stop. He was thrown over the car and landed across the road. But Peterson didn't have time to swerve.

"And he went right in through the back window of the car," says Stoehr, adding that Peterson crashed headfirst. "I think they found his teeth in the back seat."

The impact severed Peterson's nose and separated Stoehr's shoulder. Christopher Thomas Thompson, the driver of the car and a former emergency room doctor, was arrested and put on trial. The jury found him guilty of six felonies, including assault with a deadly weapon: his car. Thompson now faces 10 years in prison.

"For someone to do this to you on purpose, it's unfathomable," says Peterson, a cycling coach for the University of California, Los Angeles. He says he still can't feel his nose, he now wears false teeth, and he will forever have scars.

Drivers who kill or injure cyclists are rarely convicted.

"I'm happy that justice was served," Peterson told reporters outside the courthouse after the verdict. "I think all of our hope is that this brings to light just how vulnerable cyclists are out there."

During the trial, other cyclists told the jury of previous incidents with the driver. And a police officer testified that Thompson said he deliberately slammed on the brakes to "teach the cyclists a lesson."

"The road rage was so egregious," says *Bicycling* editor Loren Mooney. She says this may be a landmark case in protecting cyclists and pedestrians. "It's the intent, the actual road rage, that's part of the conviction in this case."

According to the National Highway Traffic Safety Administration, traffic crashes killed 716 cyclists last year and injured 52,000 people riding bikes, trikes and unicycles. That includes recent fatalities from Brookline, Mass., to Portland, Ore. But unlike the Los Angeles case, Mooney says drivers who kill or injure cyclists are rarely convicted.

"It's easy for a driver to say, 'Oh, I didn't see you. You're small, you're traveling slowly in the roadway. It was an accident,'" says Mooney. "It takes an enormous amount of evidence to get a conviction of a reckless driver, or in this case, a driver with an intent to hurt somebody with a vehicle."

Mooney says crashes often happen when drivers are distracted by cell phones, texts and other hazards. And she warns bike riders not to aggravate or escalate tensions on the road.

Driver Resentment

The Mandeville Canyon driver's reaction was perhaps an extreme example of the everyday resentment heard from other motorists.

"These bicyclists are extremely rude, and they take up the road—four, five people at a time," complained one caller to NPR member station KPCC's show *AirTalk*. The caller said he lives in Mandeville Canyon, and he has had it with cyclists.

"When you pull up alongside them and ask them to stay out of your way, they yell at you," he said. "They're extremely provocative, they're asking for trouble, and this is not the worst case that's going to happen. Someone's going to get killed, and to be frank with you, the residents aren't going to feel too bad about it."

Another Mandeville Canyon resident, Tom Freeman, is sympathetic to vulnerable cyclists. But as president of the homeowners' association, he hears complaints that when drivers try to pass bike riders, "they give them the finger."

"If they catch up with them at a stop sign, they'll kick their cars," he says. "Somebody was spit at. It's the few that cause the problems, and they help create a perception."

Cycling in Fear

East Hollywood boasts what's known as a "bicycle district," with a bike shop, cafe and bike repair co-op. Here, cycling activist Stephen Box complains that police officers don't take bike crashes seriously. And he says cyclists feel the brunt of car drivers' frustrations.

"I've been left-hooked and hit. I've been hit from behind and left in the streets," says Box. "And they expect cyclists to ride where it's unsafe: It's unsafe to ride through potholes in the gutter pan; it's unsafe to ride through broken glass in the gutter pan; it's unsafe to ride in the door zone."

His wife, Enci, says that's why cyclists often ride the way they do—to survive, even if that means sometimes running red lights.

"When I see the light turn red, I try to race as fast as I can through it," she says, "because I know I will have a block of peace and quiet, where there won't be cars behind me."

These cyclists point out that it's actually legal to ride side by side in the streets of L.A. But the rules of the road can be confusing. That's why Alex Thompson wrote what's known as the Cyclists' Bill of Rights.

"Cyclists have the right to travel safely and free of fear. We have the right to the full support of the judicial system," says Thompson, a bike blogger who also co-founded the L.A. bike cooperative Bikerowave. "These are all rights cyclists already have, but we need to reaffirm these."

But even Thompson and another bike blogger, Ted Rogers, disapprove of reckless bike riders who maneuver through traffic as if playing a video game.

"Oh, we hate these guys," says Rogers. "We absolutely hate them. The driver you tick off is the one who's going to run me off the road."

18

Cyclists Cause Road Rage

Scott Rowan

Scott Rowan is the author of The Urban Cyclist's Survival Guide *and the blog* The Urban Cyclist.

It is important that cyclists understand that they incite most of the road rage they experience by behaving rudely to others on the road. Rude cyclists might not experience a driver's rage directly, but the driver will still be fuming when they come across the next cyclist. Cyclists need to be respectful of everyone they encounter on the road, including people in automobiles.

Riding home last night from work and riding into work this morning I was stunned, yet again, at how rude some cyclists are and how their actions directly lead to injuries to other cyclists they will never meet.

While researching my new book *The Urban Cyclist's Survival Guide*, I had conversations with several experts about road rage. One of those experts was Dr. Leon James, a professor of psychology at the University of Hawaii who specializes in road rage and maintains a site about road rage at DrDriving.org.

We will touch on the topic of road rage several times in the blog. The revisiting of the topic isn't to drag out one subject and make it last for several blogs. No, the reason is that road rage is one of the most important topics for any motorist, pedestrian, trucker or cyclist trying to share the roadways with other motorists, pedestrians, truckers and cyclists.

Cyclist Behavior

What struck me about both the cyclists I experienced was their complete lack of self-awareness, especially considering that both men were dressed like Lance Armstrong-wannabes with expensive clothing to match their expensive bikes. Yet, for all the money they spent on their gear and equipment, they proved to be more of a harm to other cyclists than any angry motorist.

Why? Because the excessive and rude actions of both the cyclists provoked and antagonized the motorists around them. In short, the self-righteous actions of these two cyclists caused the road rage that other cyclists—me—had to deal with later.

I was cycling north on Clark Street [in Chicago] going home from work when I steered left in the bike lane to avoid a car door opening. To my surprise, I was nearly knocked sideways by an Armstrong-wannabe replete in special cycling-specific shorts, shirt and shoes. He never announced his presence, never tried to yell "on your left" or even ring a bell. He simply rode up from behind me and was so close to me when I avoided the car door that I saw he needed to trim his nose hair.

Cyclists are getting more and more rude to other cyclists and to motorists every ride.

I was furious and ready to say something at the next red light, pointing out that he nearly caused a wreck for both of us by not letting me know he was there. But I never got the opportunity because when a cab pulled over to pick up a passenger, Armstrong-wannabe stopped and yelled at the driver to get out of the bike lane.

I simply rode past the verbal sparring and all I could think was—*Great, now I'm riding in front of a driver who is so furious with a rude cyclist that the driver is going to run me off the road.*

Sure enough, when we got to a tight stretch of the road about a half mile further, the cab driver purposefully drove to the right side of his lane to pinch off the bike lane and force me to wait behind him. Maybe the cabbie would have done the same rude driving if a cyclist hadn't just yelled at him inches from his face. But I'm willing to bet a week's salary that Armstrong-wannabe's tirade is what caused the cab driver to squeeze me out of the bike path in his moment of road rage at the other cyclist.

I chalked that up to bad luck. But on today's commute into work I realized it wasn't bad luck, it's simply the fact that cyclists are getting more and more rude to other cyclists and to motorists every ride.

Riding into the Loop along Clark Street, I had another Armstrong-wannabe (we'll call this guy Armstrong-ain't to avoid confusion) force his way between myself and traffic at one of the worst intersections along Clark St., at the LaSalle intersection. Clark St. is pockmarked with potholes along that stretch so keeping an eye on the road is pretty important. I have no idea what exactly happened, but after forcing himself between my bike and traffic, Armstrong-ain't decided to give the middle finger to either myself or the motorist next to me. I don't know which of us he was flicking off but neither myself nor the car had done anything wrong. The only person doing anything wrong was Armstrong-ain't who thinks Clark St. is the 16th stage of the Tour De France [long-distance bicycle race through France].

Cyclists have plenty of fault to find with motorists, bus drivers and truck drivers.

But lately I've decided that the worst enemy of most cyclists are other cyclists who act in such ridiculous and anger-provoking ways that they only do harm to other cyclists. After all, when Armstrong-wannabe and Armstrong-ain't have turned onto another street during their ride, they may have forgotten about yelling at the cab driver or giving the finger to other motorists, but those car drivers haven't forgotten. Road rage festers and burns, it doesn't just fade away. And when those drivers interact with another cyclist they are not going to have any thoughts of civility toward dealing with them, uh I mean, us.

That means the real reason behind so much road rage is actually bicyclists themselves who ride like they're protected on high from Keyser Soze [a fictional character in the 1995 film *The Usual Suspects*]. They are not. None of us are. And the last thing I need is dealing with a road rage incident caused by a thoughtless cyclist who is the one who deserves all the blame for causing the road rage by simply acting like a jerk.

We were all told to learn to play well with others when we were children. The adage doesn't change now that we're adults. And it's even more vital for cyclists to drop their self-important demeanor and attitude when dealing with traffic because cyclists cause more road rage incidents than they suffer. They're just too self-absorbed to acknowledge it.

Organizations to Contact

The editors have compiled the following list of organizations concerned with the issues debated in this book. The descriptions are derived from materials provided by the organizations. All have publications or information available for interested readers. The list was compiled on the date of publication of the present volume; names, addresses, phone and fax numbers, and e-mail and Internet addresses may change. Be aware that many organizations take several weeks or longer to respond to inquiries, so allow as much time as possible.

AAA Foundation for Traffic Safety
607 14th St. NW, Suite 201, Washington, DC   20005
(202) 638-5944 • fax: (202) 638-5943
e-mail: info@aaafoundation.org
website: www.aaafoundation.org

The AAA Foundation for Traffic Safety was founded to conduct research to address growing highway safety issues. The organization's mission is to identify traffic safety problems, foster research that seeks solutions, and disseminate information and educational materials. The Foundation has funded over 250 projects designed to discover the causes of traffic crashes, prevent them, and minimize injuries when they do occur. The Foundation's materials, many of which are available on their website, seek to give drivers new skills, sharpen old ones, and change attitudes as the first step to changing behaviors. The group's website includes a number of articles, reports, and videos dealing with the subject of road rage.

Center for Problem-Oriented Policing (POP Center)
website: www.popcenter.org/problems/aggressive_driving

The mission of the Center for Problem-Oriented Policing (POP Center) is to advance the concept and practice of problem-oriented policing in open and democratic societies. It does so by making readily accessible information about ways in which police can more effectively address specific crime and disorder problems. The POP Center is a nonprofit organization comprising affiliated police practitioners, researchers, and universities dedicated to the advancement of problem-oriented policing. The POP Center website has curriculum guides, teaching aids, problem analysis tools, and an immense range of information on a variety of topics, including aggressive driving.

Federal Motor Carrier Safety Administration (FMCSA)

1200 New Jersey Ave. SE, Washington, DC   20590
(800) 832-5660
website: www.fmcsa.dot.gov

The Federal Motor Carrier Safety Administration (FMCSA) was established within the US Department of Transportation, pursuant to the Motor Carrier Safety Improvement Act of 1999. Formerly a part of the Federal Highway Administration, the FMCSA's primary mission is to prevent commercial motor vehicle-related fatalities and injuries. Activities of the Administration contribute to ensuring safety in motor carrier operations through strong enforcement of safety regulations; targeting high-risk carriers and commercial motor vehicle drivers; improving safety information systems and commercial motor vehicle technologies; strengthening commercial motor vehicle equipment and operating standards; and increasing safety awareness. Their website contains a section devoted to road rage for commercial drivers.

Governors Highway Safety Association (GHSA)

444 N. Capitol St. NW, Suite 722
Washington, DC   20001-1534
(202) 789-0942 • fax: (202) 789-0946
e-mail: headquarters@ghsa.org
website: www.ghsa.org

The Governors Highway Safety Association (GHSA) is a nonprofit representing the state and territorial highway safety offices that implement programs to address behavioral highway safety issues. GHSA provides leadership and advocacy for the states and territories to improve traffic safety, influence national policy, enhance program management, and promote best practices. The group's website includes links to their publications, including the "2013 Distracted Driving: Survey of the States" report. A portion of the website is also dedicated to the topic of speeding and aggressive driving.

Insurance Institute for Highway Safety (IIHS)/Highway Loss Data Institute (HLDI)

1005 N. Glebe Rd., Suite 800, Arlington, VA 22201
(703) 247-1500 • fax: (703) 247-1588
website: www.carsafety.org

The Insurance Institute for Highway Safety (IIHS) is an independent, nonprofit scientific and educational organization dedicated to reducing the losses—deaths, injuries, and property damage—from crashes on the nation's roads. The Highway Loss Data Institute (HLDI) shares and supports this mission through scientific studies of insurance data representing the human and economic losses resulting from the ownership and operation of different types of vehicles and by publishing insurance loss results by vehicle make and model. Their joint website contains information on road rage statistics.

National Highway Traffic Safety Administration (NHTSA)

1200 New Jersey Ave. SE, West Building
Washington, DC 20590
(888) 327-4236
website: www.nhtsa.gov

The National Highway Traffic Safety Administration (NHTSA), established by the Highway Safety Act of 1970, is dedicated to achieving the highest standards of excellence in motor vehicle and highway safety. It works daily to help prevent crashes and their attendant costs, both human and financial. The website includes press releases, current research, and information on all of their programs as well as a special section devoted to the topic of aggressive driving with guides, planners, and information to aid law enforcement professionals and prosecutors in the reduction of aggressive driving.

National Safety Council (NSC)

1121 Spring Lake Dr., Itasca, IL   60143-3201
(800) 621-7615 • fax: (630) 285-1315
website: www.nsc.org

The National Safety Council (NSC) is a nonprofit organization whose mission is to save lives by preventing injuries and deaths at work, in homes and communities, and on the road through leadership, research, education, and advocacy. NSC advances this mission by partnering with businesses, government agencies, elected officials, and the public to make an impact where the most preventable injuries and deaths occur—in areas such as distracted driving, teen driving, workplace safety, and beyond the workplace, particularly in and near our homes. The NSC website includes a section titled "Safety on the Road" containing specific information on the topics of defensive driving, distracted driving, and teen driving.

Reaching Out Against Road Rage (R.O.A.R.R.)

website: www.roarrinc.org

Reaching Out Against Road Rage (R.O.A.R.R.) is a nonprofit organization designed to fight the growing danger of road rage along the highways and byways of the United States. To combat this public threat, R.O.A.R.R. intends to improve traffic safety through public awareness of the road rage problem, and then continue to work towards the solution to road rage through education. On their website, the group produces and provides educational tools to help communities reduce the destructive impact of road rage.

Bibliography

Books

Christine A.
Adamec

Impulse Control Disorders. New York: Chelsea House, 2008.

Barry Glassner

The Culture of Fear: Why Americans Are Afraid of the Wrong Things—Crime, Drugs, Minorities, Teen Moms, Killer Kids, Mutant Microbes, Plane Crashes, Road Rage, & So Much More, rev. ed. New York: Basic Books, 2010.

Brian Ladd

Autophobia: Love and Hate in the Automotive Age. Chicago: University of Chicago Press, 2008.

Yusheng Lin

Aggressive Driving: Insights Derived from Psychology's General Aggression Model. El Paso, TX: LFB Scholarly Publishing, 2013.

Lawrence Ribeiro

The Unknown Art of Driving: An Ultimate Guide for Any Driver for Any Situation or Environment. Los Angeles: Lawrence Ribeiro, 2013.

Periodicals and Internet Sources

Suneel M.
Agerwala et al.

"Aggressive Driving in Young Motorists," *International Journal of Humanities and Social Sciences,* Fall 2008.

F. Javier Alvarez, Inmaculada Fierro, and Claudia Morales	"Alcohol Use, Illicit Drug Use, and Road Rage," *Journal of Studies on Alcohol and Drugs*, March 2011.
John Barnes	"Distracted Drivers: Taking Their Toll on the Roads," MLive.com, February 1, 2012.
Tammy Stables Battaglia	"600 Pulled Over for Aggressive Driving on Metro Detroit Freeways," *Detroit Free Press*, July 26, 2013. www.freep.com.
Melissa Nann Burke	"Delaware Latest to Take Aim at Left-Lane Dawdlers," *The News Journal*, April 19, 2012.
Joe Cardona	"Critical Mass Cycling in Miami a Mix of Protest, Party," *Miami Herald*, August 16, 2013. www.miamiherald.com.
CBS News	"Road Rage Considered Brain Disorder," February 11, 2009. www.cbsnews.com.
Jill Craig	"Kenyan Minibus Driver Seeks to Unionize to Stop Road Rage," Voice of America, October 29, 2012. www.voanews.com.
Dennis Gaffney	"This Guy Can Get 59 MPG in a Plain Old Accord. Beat That, Punk," *Mother Jones*, January/February 2007.

Michael Graczyk	"Financial Analyst Turned 'Road Rage Killer' to Be Executed in Texas," *Business Insider*, July 30, 2013. www.businessinsider.com.
Emanuella Grinberg	"Air Rage: Passengers 'Quicker to Snap,'" CNN, June 1, 2012. www.cnn.com.
Bob Gritzinger	"Hypermiling Rewards Are Just Not Worth the Risks," *AutoWeek*, June 17, 2009. www.autoweek.com.
Leon James	"The Psychology of Pedestrian Rage," DrDriving.org, 2007.
Michael O'Reilly	"What to Do When Road Rage Finds You," *The Sydney Morning Herald*, July 29, 2013. www.smh.com.au.
John Rafferty	"Road Rage: Stop Delaying; Time to Act Is Now," *Courier Times*, August 6, 2013. www.phillyburbs.com.
David Sands	"Detroit Critical Mass Helps Area Cyclists Find Common Ground on City Streets," *Huffington Post*, April 27, 2012. www.huffingtonpost.com.
Tom Stafford	"The Psychology of Why Cyclists Enrage Car Drivers," BBC, February 12, 2013. www.bbc.com.
Maia Szalavitz	"Sidewalk Rage: Mental Illness or 'Altruistic Punishment?'" February 17, 2011. http://healthland.time.com.

John C. Umhau
et al.

"The Physician's Unique Role in
Preventing Violence: A Neglected
Opportunity?" *BMC Medicine*,
November 2012.

Shirley S. Wang

"Get Out of My Way, You Jerk!" *Wall
Street Journal*, February 15, 2011.
http://online.wsj.com.

Index